THE GIRL'S GUIDE TO
Surfing

by **ANDREA McCLOUD**

illustrations by **SYMBOLON**

THE GIRL'S GUIDE TO Surfing

CHRONICLE BOOKS
SAN FRANCISCO

Text copyright © 2005 by Andrea McCloud.
Illustrations copyright © 2005 by Symbolon.
All rights reserved. No part of this book may be reproduced in any
form without written permission from the publisher.

Library of Congress Cataloging-in-Publication Data available.

ISBN-13: 978-0-8118-4645-5
ISBN-10: 0-8118-4645-8

Manufactured in China
Designed by Vivien Sung
Typeset in Trade Gothic, Century Expanded, Clarendon Condensed,
    Nobel, Antique Central, Tiki Holiday, and Tiki Hut

10 9 8 7 6 5 4

Chronicle Books LLC
680 Second Street
San Francisco, California 94107

www.chroniclebooks.com

DEDICATION

To the kook in all of us.

ACKNOWLEDGMENTS

I am beholden to all of the surfers who contributed to this book for their invaluable insights, suggestions, and stories. Special thanks to my editor, Sarah Malarkey, for her enthusiasm and guidance; to illustrator Symbolon, for creating such strong and sexy surfers; and to surf guru Matt Warshaw for a very—*very*—thorough fact-check (he did write the encyclopedia on the subject, after all). I'd also like to thank the team at Chronicle Books, especially designer Vivien Sung, for all of their hard work on the project. And above all, ever-lasting appreciation goes to Derek Gaertner, my main man and surf sensei: I couldn't have done it without you.

CONTENTS

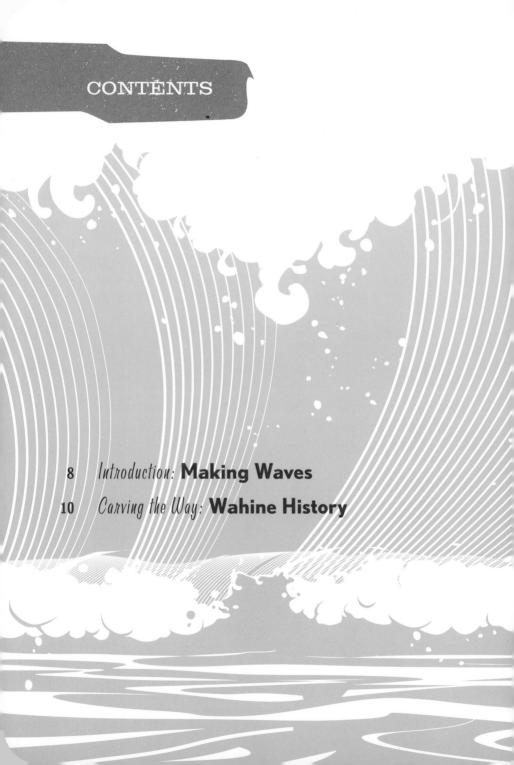

✦ Introduction: Making Waves

FROM MALIBU, California, to Narragansett, Rhode Island, from Tofino, British Columbia, to Cornwall, England, women are carving turns in record numbers. Though women have been surfing for hundreds of years, it's really only been since the early 1990s that our presence in the sport has begun to receive its rightful due. And thanks to the dedication of past and current wahines things are continuing to change. True, most lineups are still dominated by men. True, male pros still earn roughly ten times that of female pros. True, it's really hard to find a decent pair of women's trunks. But what's also true is that every year more and more ladies are making the charge, and every year—through the tenacity of the pros and the ambition of aspiring surfers like you—the sport of surfing is opening its arms to women. "The barriers are starting to fall," says veteran surfer Rochelle Ballard. "There is a lot more common ground in the water because we're multiplying and the men are more comfortable because they see more and more women in the lineup. The majority of the guys are starting to realize that we have just as much joy for surfing as they do, and that we kind of lighten up the lineup and bring a real grace to surfing."

Surfing is a physical, emotional, and soulful experience. It's you and you alone using your mind, your body, and your spirit to synchronously move with the rhythm of the ocean, to harmoniously ride its explosions of energy. In two words: sheer exhilaration, or perhaps more aptly put, totally awesome. It takes strength, endurance, and balance, both physical and mental; it takes stamina, commitment, and patience; but most of all, it takes the courage to get out there. Being a beginner at anything is tough and humbling, but especially so with surfing, where just about everything, from buying a wetsuit to carrying your board to the beach to entering the surf zone, can be intimidating and challenging. But if you have courage, the rest will come with time and (lots of) practice.

The practice factor is something that cannot be emphasized enough. Though many of the people in the lineup make surfing look easy, it most likely took them years—yes, years—to master. And you, just like everyone else, will have to go through that same humbling and sometimes painful evolution from kook to full-fledged surfer. Realize it may take months for you to catch your first bona fide wave; don't get discouraged—it's difficult for everybody. Bottom line: If you make a commitment to surfing, you will learn to surf. It won't be pretty and you will undoubtedly get frustrated, but have faith. All of the nasty wipeouts and embarrassing moments will be worth it when you finally have that first triumphant ride to shore.

"Have fun with it because that's the main reason you should be surfing. Don't be hard on yourself. A lot of girls are insecure about something, whether it's their body or their ability, what the boys are going to think, what people are going to say. Be real with yourself," urges surf star Serena Brooke, "Say, 'Look, this is who I am, I'm not perfect, I'm not great at it, I'm a beginner and I accept that I'm learning.' Everyone has to start somewhere. Don't get ahead of yourself—enjoy the journey. Slow down and have fun with it for what it is. Don't be attached to the outcome, just enjoy the process and what it is in that moment, even if that is going over the falls and eating crap. Just laugh at yourself and keep it light."

A surfer's journey, though challenging, is ridiculously fun and rewarding. Be patient, be persistent, and surf as much as you can. This guide was designed to help you get started and to answer any questions that might arise as you improve, but there's really no substitute for getting out there and getting wet. It will take time for you to get to know your board and the ocean, and for your body to get used to surfing. You may be sore for a while or acquire the occasional bump or bruise—that's all part of it. Take pride in these beautiful battle wounds and stick with it.

CHARGE!

✦ Carving the Way: **Wahine History**

✦ Leslie Lemon, Marion Dowsett, and Beatrice Dowsett, all from Hawaii, are among the first ladies to tandem with Duke.

✦ Beatrice Newport is touted as the best female surfer in Waikiki.

✦ California's Mary Ann Hawkins is the surfing powerhouse of the late 1930s and 1940s.

✦ Hawaii's Ethel Kukea and Malibu's Vickie Flaxman, Robin Grigg, and Aggie Bane dominate women's surfing in the mid to late 1950s. ↪

A VERY, VERY LONG TIME AGO

✦ Pele, legendary Hawaiian goddess of volcanoes, learns to surf and teaches her sister Hi'iaka.

✦ Mamala, Hawaiian O'ahu chief and demigod, inspires audiences with her surfing skills and supernatural powers.

EARLY 1900S

✦ Hawaiians Mildred Turner and Josephine Pratt are admitted to the Hui Nalu surfing/canoeing club, established by Duke Kahanamoku, the founding father of modern surfing.

✦ Isabel Letham numbers among Australia's original surfers.

1700S AND 1800S

✦ Polynesian women charge regularly alongside the men.

10

- Marge Calhoun, from California, is *the* female surfing presence of the late 1950s and early 1960s.
- The book *Gidget* is released in 1957, becomes a best seller, and is followed two years later by the movie of the same name; women's surfing hits the mainstream.
- In 1959, California's Linda Benson, five-time U.S. champion and one of the first female nose-riders and hotdoggers, becomes the first woman to surf the massive waves at Waimea Bay.

1960S

- Australia's Phyllis O'Donnell, winner of the 1964 world title, and Gail Couper, five-time national champion, are the major influences from Down Under.
- Hawaiian Joyce Hoffman wins the world championships in 1965 and 1966, and is the first woman to surf Pipeline.

1970S

- Margo Godfrey Oberg (California/Hawaii), four-time world champion, wins her first world title at age fifteen and remains a dominating force on the pro surf scene for over ten years; she is also touted as the best female big-wave rider.
- Lynne Boyer (New Jersey/Hawaii) wins two world titles and is far and away the flashiest female surfer of the decade.
- Hawaii's Rell Sunn, Sally Prange, Patti Paniccia, Claudia Bates, →

+ In 1991, Quicksilver launches a junior girl's line, Roxy; Roxy introduces the first ever girl's board short in 1993; the following year Roxy begins its sponsorship of pro surfers and events.

+ In 2003 MTV airs its reality TV series, *Surf Girls,* and the WB launches its reality-based show, *Boarding House: North Shore,* bringing women's surfing into thousands of homes across the country.

Shortboarders

+ California's Lisa Andersen wins four world titles and makes the cover of *Surfer* magazine with the splash title "Lisa Andersen surfs better than you." ➼

1970S (CONTINUED)

and Becky Benson and Californian Jericho Poppler join the men's tour of South Africa and Brazil, forming the core of the first women's pro tour. Mary Setterholm (California) and Poppler found the Women's International Surfing Association (WISA), the first all-women's pro circuit; their first event is held in San Onofre.

1980S

+ Association of Surfing Professionals (ASP) is formed and begins overseeing the men's and women's pro circuits.

+ Pam Burridge becomes Australia's first full-time female pro and later wins one world title. ➼

+ Floridian Frieda Zamba, four-time world champion and the youngest woman to win an ASP pro event, dominates the pro circuit for ten years, along with South Africa's Wendy Botha, who also wins four world titles.

Longboarders

+ California's Kim Hamrock, winner of one world longboard title, is the first and so far only woman to charge Puerto Escondito with the boys in the annual Central Surf Longboard Invitational.

+ Hawaii's Daize Shayne, two-time longboarding world champion, continues to dazzle audiences with her style and charisma. She brings major media attention to women's longboarding.

+ Hawaii's Rochelle Ballard distinguishes herself as the premier female tuberider.

+ Australian Layne Beachley, six-time world champion and big-wave master, is the queen of tow-in surfing.

+ Sarah Gerhardt of California is the first woman to ride the colossal waves at Maverick's. ➡

THE FUTURE

Shortboarders

+ Hawaii's Keala Kennelly is arguably the best female barrel rider of all time.

+ Australia's Chelsea Georgeson, 2002 ASP Rookie of the Year, is a quickly rising star.

+ Peruvian Sofia Mulanovich has the attitude and fortitude of a true champion. ➡

Longboarders

+ Californian Kassia Meador, voted by *Surfer* magazine (April 2002) as one of the top ten up-and-comer female longboarders, is the first woman to post a perfect score against the men at the 2001 Hebridean Surfing Festival off the Isle of Lewis, Scotland.

+ Oahu's Joy Magelssen is another up-and-comer to watch.

Chapter 1:
Wave Breakdown

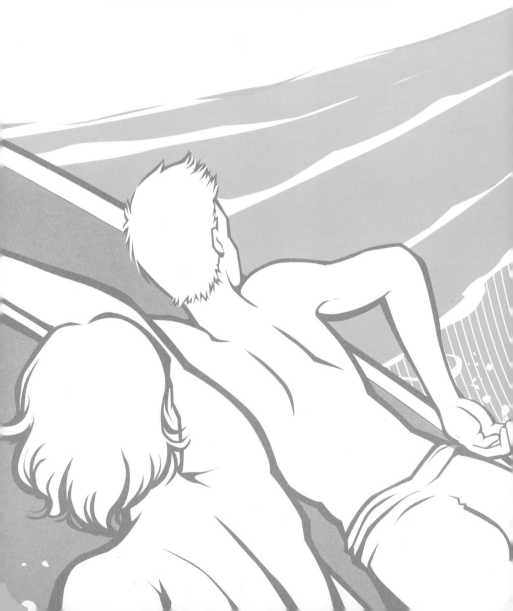

✦ THE BIRTH OF SURF:
SWELL TO WAVE

Put simply, waves are caused by wind blowing across the ocean's surface. A strong wind will first form small patches of chop. As the wind continues to blow over the water's surface, the chop combines and recombines to form wavelets. These wavelets then merge with other small waves to create larger waves. As these larger waves travel over long distances, they move farther apart from each other and become smoother, cleaner, more organized waves called *swell* (the long, graceful, uninterrupted lines of energy that you see rolling into shore). The size of the swell depends on the wind's intensity, duration, and *fetch* (the distance along the water's surface over which the wind blows). It may sound technical, but it's actually pretty straightforward—greater intensity, longer duration, and wider fetch equal bigger swells. A swell can travel for thousands of miles before it hits the shore, drags on the ocean bottom, and forms a bona fide breaking wave (aka surf). Just what shape these waves take depends a lot on swell direction, size, and speed; currents; tide; local wind; and the contour of the ocean bottom.

Shop•talk:

You may hear the word *swell* being tossed around with relative frequency. An example: "There's a swell coming on Wednesday!" Don't
get confused—for the most part, there is usually some sort of swell,
though perhaps small, in the water. This particular phraseology is
surf-speak for "There's a *bigger* swell coming on Wednesday,"
which equates to *bigger* waves hitting the shore. Make a mental
note, and on Wednesday choose your surf spot wisely. Some breaks
are more open to the swell than others; find the one with waves that
are the appropriate size for your skill level. (For forecasting conditions, see page 29.)

Shop•talk:

A group of bigger-than-average waves rolling toward shore is
called a *set*. The downtime between sets (the time you ideally want
to paddle out to the lineup; see page 73) is called a *lull*.

the evolution of surf: from chop to wave

windswell: Born of more localized winds that have just enough fetch and blow just long enough to form rideable waves. Often messy, lumpy, and disorganized.

groundswell: Formed by very strong, distant winds. The most powerful and well defined of the swells. Travels long distances. Big wave potential.

THE WAVE FROM HEAD TO TOE

face: The front of a wave.

section: A piece of the curl line that drops down ahead of the main area of whitewater.

shoulder: The upper, unbroken part of the wave.

wall: The area of the wave face that has yet to break.

lip: The very tip of a cresting wave that's rolling or curling down.

peak: The highest part of the wave and where the wave first breaks.

trough: The bottom portion of a wave.

pocket: The steep area just ahead of the breaking section of the wave; usually where you want to position yourself and your board.

curl: The cresting, breaking part of the wave that "curls" down toward the trough; similar to "lip."

whitewater: The frothy, white part of the wave after it has broken.

Shop•talk:

You may hear people in the lineup say, "Did you make that *section*?" Translation: Were you able to get around a critical part of the wave (maybe a fast-peeling section or a particularly slow section), return to the pocket, and gloriously finish your ride?

WAVE FACE

section

lip

curl

wall

pocket

whitewater

trough

easily double-overhead

Decoding *Shape*

For better or worse, the shape of the waves will drastically influence the quality of your ride. See below for the particulars.

mushy: Waves usually formed when the ocean bottom rises gradually from deep to shallow water. Mushy waves are gently sloped, less powerful, and very forgiving—ideal for beginners.

peeling: Well-shaped waves created by a bend in the coastline (a point) or a bend in the ocean's bottom (a reef, a sand bar). This type of wave breaks successively down its face ("peels") as it rolls toward shore, delivering lots of open wave face to surf—wave perfection.

closeout: This type of wave occurs when the swell hits a uniform ocean bottom dead on, forcing the entire wave to break at once into a blanket of frothy whitewater. Closeouts in general aren't much fun for a more advanced surfer (no surfable wall), but are just fine for a beginner. Upside: no crowd.

mushy

peeling

reform: Waves created when there's a deep trench connecting two shallower sections of ocean bottom. The wave breaks, hits the trench, transforms back to a swell as it passes through deep water, then hits the second shallow section, and starts to break again. The original wave and the second "reform" wave are both potentially surfable.

double-up: A bigger, steeper, thicker breaking wave formed when two smaller waves merge. Double-ups occur when two swells overlap, or when there's a severe shift from deeper to shallower water.

hollow: Waves most often formed when there's a sudden change from deep to shallow water. The curl pitches forward and down to create a steep, "hollow" wave also known as a barrel, or tube. This wave is fast moving, powerful, and for advanced surfers only.

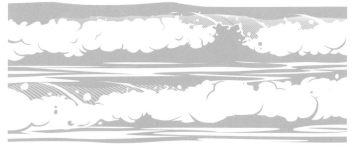

closeout

hollow

Finding oneself on the inside of a tubing wave—piped, barreled, pitted, shacked, slotted, and of course, tubed—is every surfer's dream. This crowning achievement, the ultimate in surfing, transcends skill. Beyond the grasp of the technical, you'll also need superhero-like confidence, composure, and courage.

Rochelle Ballard on being in the barrel:

" To me getting BARRELED is the most exciting part of surfing because it encompasses everything that is surfing.

IT'S LIKE BEING INSIDE THE CENTER OF EVERYTHING, INSIDE THE LIQUID ENERGY OF THE WAVE,

and that is what surfing is all about. It comes together in that moment and you're surrounded by all of this water in this still, quiet place, where time slows down . . . There's nothing better. **"**

Sizing *It Up*

Wave size is articulated by most surfers as roughly one-half to two-thirds the actual wave-face height. Assessing the actual size firsthand is easy, but translating second-hand descriptions like small, medium, and big is an entirely different story—subjectivity at its finest. While your friend Judy, a new surfer, may think that a three-foot wave is simply huge, Joey, your neighbor and ten-year surf veteran, would probably label that same wave an "ankle-slapper." When checking the surf size, it's best to go with the word of a trusted friend or to call the surf or buoy report (see "The Buoy Report," page 24, or "The Surf Report," page 29). Or better yet, go see for yourself. If you're at the beach, look for someone who's already surfing and compare his or her height with the height of the wave. That should give you a pretty good indication of the wave's true size. And remember, it usually feels bigger than it looks once you're out there, so be prepared.

shop•talk:

If the wave comes to your shoulder, it's *shoulder-high*; to the top of your head, *head-high*; over your head, *overhead*; and if it's—gasp!—twice your size, you can correctly say *double-overhead*.

MONSTER MANIA: TEN HUGE WAVES

- ✦ Avalanche, France
- ✦ Easter Reef, Victoria, Australia
- ✦ Jaws, Maui, Hawaii
- ✦ Sunset Beach, Oahu, Hawaii
- ✦ Mavericks, California
- ✦ Nazare, Portugal
- ✦ Outer Log Cabins, Oahu, Hawaii
- ✦ Puerto Escondido, Mexico
- ✦ Todos Santos, Baja, Mexico
- ✦ Waimea Bay, Oahu, Hawaii

" Puerto Escondido is one of the HEAVIEST WAVES I HAVE EVER RIDDEN. I have been the only female contestant for the four years they have held the Central Surf Longboard Invitational and I am returning this September. The men in this event are some of the very best longboarders in the world and I am honored to surf with them. Really, I am taking lessons and trying to improve my tube-riding skills. I learn more every year and find this wave extremely challenging. NOT FOR THE FAINT OF HEART! My hope is to see that I have inspired one of the local Mexican girls to go out there and CHARGE LIKE NO OTHER GIRL EVER BEFORE . . . "

THE BUOY REPORT

A buoy report, which you can get from your local weather service or various online sites, gives you measurements of open-ocean swell. It provides three very valuable pieces of information: wave height, wave period, and swell direction. Understanding these factors coupled with an understanding of your local break will eventually help you to better determine the size and condition of the surf on any given day.

wave height: The measurement of a wave from trough to peak as the swell moves through open ocean. The size of the waves as you see them from the beach may be bigger or smaller than this initial figure depending on the ocean bottom and the wave period.

wave period: The time interval (in seconds) between two successive wave crests as they pass a stationary point, usually a buoy, on the ocean surface. This number will give you a good indication of the swell's energy, speed, and organization: The larger the period, the more powerful and organized the swell. This often-overlooked factor can have a huge impact on the wave sizes you see from the beach. Let's say you have two swells, both with a 6-foot wave height. The first swell has an 18-second period, which could easily translate to ten-foot or greater surf, while the second swell, with only an 8-second period, could show surf as small as 3 or 4 feet.

swell direction: The direction from which the swell originates (listed in degrees, east: 90, south: 180, west: 270, and north: 360). The size and shape of the waves that hit your beach will greatly depend on the orientation of your break and the swell direction. If the swell originates in the south and your beach faces south, generally speaking, you'll receive the full energy of the swell, i.e., bigger waves; however if that same swell hits a beach that faces west or northwest, for example, it will need to wrap into the beach, often losing significant amounts of energy and decreasing the wave size.

✦ THE BREAKS

Beach *break*

At a *beachbreak*, the swell hits a sandbar, which then forces the wave to break. Because sandbars readily shift, the wave shapes at a beachbreak can be inconsistent, erratic, and unpredictable. More often than not, these waves break quickly and very close to shore, and they tend to be steeper and hollower (though there are exceptions). Because of their speed and slope, most beachbreaks are best suited for the more maneuverable short board.

beachbreak

Point *break*

A bend in the coastline can create a *pointbreak*. This bend causes an approaching wave to wrap around the point and peel successively down its face as it rolls toward shore. Pointbreaks are ideal for surfing because the wave shape is consistent and has a lot of open face to surf.

Reef *break*

Reefbreaks are surf spots where the waves break over a rock or coral reef. Because the bottom is stationary, reefbreaks create consistently shaped waves (unlike a beachbreak, where the sand is constantly being shifted). And because reefbreaks tend to create an abrupt change from deep to shallow water, they are home to some of the most famous barrels in the world.

pointbreak

The direction a wave is breaking is observed while on the wave, looking at the beach. A wave that breaks to the left and that you ride to the left is called a *left*. Likewise, a wave that breaks to the right and that you ride to the right is called a *right*. In a beachside conversation you might say, "Check out that left," or "That right is screaming my name."

✦THE ELEMENTS

Local *Wind*

The local wind—that is, wind conditions over or near a given surf break—can greatly affect the quality of the surf. Some days the surf will be *glassy*, i.e., windless, clean and smooth, while other days you will be sidelined because it is a windy, bumpy, *blown-out* mess. Generally speaking, the morning or early evening, when there is usually little or no wind, is the best time to surf, so if you're up for dawn patrol or a sunset session, you should hit it. Otherwise, be on the look out for *offshore* wind—it's a beautiful thing. It blows from the beach onto the surf and can greatly improve the shape of the waves (a telltale sign: mist spraying seaward off the lip of a cresting wave). Not to be confused with its evil sibling, *onshore wind*, which blows from the ocean onto shore. Onshore wind usually indicates abysmal surf conditions and is our enemy. And finally, though not quite as ruthless as onshore wind, *side-shore wind*, wind that blows across the waves, can also equate to unpleasant (but bearable) conditions.

Tides

The ocean's tides are created primarily by the gravitational pull of the moon. They generally go from high to low (or vice versa) in about six hours. A full tidal cycle usually takes just over twelve hours to complete. A shoreline's appearance can drastically change with the switching tides. (Expect tides to have their greatest swings at full or no moon.) Where once there were lapping waves and a narrow beach you may now find exposed rocks and clamoring crabs. Likewise, tides also drastically change surf conditions. Some spots are clearly better on a high tide, some show their true colors on a low tide, and others shine the most brightly on a changing tide. It's a good idea to find out which tide is the optimal for your surf spot. Ask around or see for yourself.

THE SURF REPORT

Some surf shops have a hotline that will give you a daily surf report (tides, size, wind conditions). It may be a recording or it may just be an employee who went out that morning and can tell you with some authority if the surf was any good. If you don't live near the coast, make sure to program this number into your speed dial—it can save you an unnecessary trip to the beach. And if you have access to the Internet, you can also easily check the surf (at your home break or just about anywhere in the world!) as well as the buoy report, any upcoming storms, hurricanes, tidal charts, and other weather conditions at the premier surf forecaster and much-appreciated www.surfline.com. Several similar sites include www.buoyweather.com, www.stormsurf.com, and the U.S. Navy's meteorology and oceanography center, https://www.fnmoc.navy.mil/. Not only do these sites provide a written description of conditions, but many of them also host twenty-four-hour live surf-cams, which allow you to actually *see* the surf from the comfort of your home.

Chapter 2: **Gear**

✦ THE SURF SHOP

Where there's a popular beach, there's a surf shop; hit the one closest to your chosen surf locale, and if there's more than one, give them all a look-see. The surf shop is the Shangri-la of surfing accoutrement. Packed with everything and anything you could possibly need to surf, it's the perfect spot to begin and nurture your surfing career. And to boot, the sales force is usually comprised of seasoned surfers who *know* their gear and can help you make wise equipment choices for your size and ability. Spend some time cruising the aisles. Make friends. Don't be embarrassed and do not be afraid to ask questions. Most of these guys will be more than happy to impress you with their vast knowledge of surfing and its ever-evolving accessories. You may even get a free lesson out of it. The gear can get a bit expensive and you don't want to get stuck with the wrong fit, so always make sure you do your research before you make any serious investments.

✦ YOUR FIRST BOARD

There's a lot to know about surfboards, and in time, you will learn it all, but right now, if you're choosing your first board, you really need to keep in mind just two words: *big* and *fat*. As a newcomer to the sport, you are simply looking for a board that nurtures some confidence, and for a green surfer, that's a tank. Think sedan. No, think Cadillac.

Soft *board*

A polyethylene-covered soft board is a great option for a beginner. Plain and simple: They are safer. These boards are much softer than fiberglass-wrapped boards and have round edges, so it's not quite as painful if you get bonked on the head, (though your pride may be bruised). The only drawback: They're a bit sluggish in the water, and they scream rookie (although this is going to be pretty obvious anyway). After your first few sessions, you may be eager to try a fiberglass board.

I'd say rent one, and if you decide surfing is for you, spend some money for the real thing.

Long board

Many people begin their surfing career on what's called a longboard, typically around 9 feet long, 23 inches wide, and 3 inches thick, with a rounded nose, wide tail, and trifin or single-fin configuration. The thickness makes the board more buoyant, while the length, width, and rounded nose increase stability. These boards are easier to paddle than shortboards, easier to sit on, and make it easier to catch and ride waves. If you go with a longboard, a word of caution: make sure you pick one that fits securely under your arm (you can firmly grip the rail) and can be carried comfortably. Full-size longboards can be too wide or too heavy for a petite woman. Hold a few and see how they feel. You may find that a board 21 inches wide, instead of 23 inches, is more appropriate, or you may find that the traditional width is just perfect. Spend some time making your decision, it's an expensive one—these boards, any new boards for that matter, are not cheap.

WISE BUYS

Buying just any old board is a bad idea. Put a real effort into your search and make sure you choose the right board for you skill level. Many beginners have abandoned surfing altogether because they had the wrong board but didn't know it. (We can't all be like former world champion Pauline Menczer, who learned how to surf on half of her brother's broken surfboard!) Learning to surf is hard enough; make it easier on yourself by starting with the appropriate equipment.

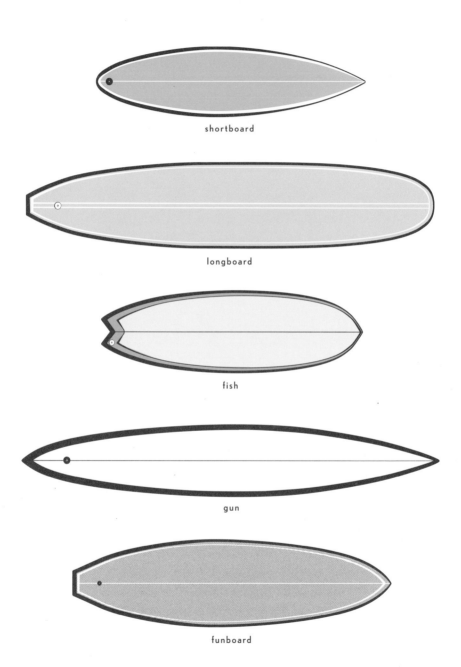

shortboard

longboard

fish

gun

funboard

Fun *board*

Funboards usually run from about 7 to 8 feet. They're similar to longboards, but a bit shorter, thinner, narrower, with a slightly pointier nose. A funboard is a hybrid of the shortboard and longboard; while it gives you a certain amount of longboard stability, it introduces the maneuverability of a shortboard. Funboards are almost always trifins, and are good for people who want to eventually evolve to shortboarding (see "To Rip: Shortboarding Basics," page 94). They are harder to learn on but will make for a smoother transition from a longer board to a shorter board if that's your goal.

SECONDHAND STICK

You might consider buying a used board. Most surf shops sell secondhand boards, or you can snoop around neighborhood garage sales or check the newspaper, your local online community (www.craigslist.org is a good place to start), or eBay. A word of caution, however: Take a board-savvy friend along—you don't want to get stuck with a dog. And before you buy anything, give it a thorough once-over to ensure it's in good condition and doesn't have any substantial dings (i.e., holes, water damage to foam, cracks in the fiberglass around the nose, tail, or fins, or delamination).

THE BRO DEAL

Usually when you buy a new board, shops will throw in a leash, a few bars of wax, and some choice stickers for free (my male friends call it "the bro deal"; I call it "necessary appreciation" because I just threw down five hundred bucks at your shop). If this option is not initially offered to you (it does help if you're a frequent patron of the shop), it doesn't hurt to ask.

✦ BOARD TLC

Salt water as well as the sun can cause serious damage to your board; always rinse it off with fresh water after surfing and stick it in a shady spot, or better yet, in your board bag in a shady spot. If it's hot outside, don't leave your board to bake in your car—melted wax is really messy and a royal pain to clean up, and worse, the intense heat can lead to board delamination. When you get a ding, repair it as soon as possible (see "Ding Repair," below). If the damage is too great for you to handle yourself, take it to a pro. A good repair job can be expensive but is invaluable to the life of your board. And please, *please*, don't set your vulnerable board next to or behind your car—*crunch!*—or lean it up vertically against a wall—slide, scrape, *wahbam!*

Ding Repair

Board dings (a puncture or crack in the fiberglass) are an annoying reality of surfing; at some point, perhaps while surfing over a rock bottom, or more likely, while you are carrying your board down a narrow staircase, your board will invariably get a ding. If the ding occurs while you're surfing, first allow the board to thoroughly dry, and then do the repairs. Make sure you fix the ding before the board gets wet again—you *don't* want water leaking into the board's inner foam. Though they are a pain, minor dings are relatively easy to fix.

What You'll Need Ding repair kits are available at any respectable surf shop, or you can make your own. A good kit should include wet/dry sandpaper (80, 120, and 220 grit), a sanding block, 4-oz fiberglass cloth, resin (get the stuff that cures in the sun—I suggest Suncure or Quick Fix), filler-resin (different from regular resin, also buy the brands that cure in the sun), scissors, and surgical gloves. An old credit card is optional.

1. Make sure the dinged area is completely, *completely* dry.
2. Put on a long sleeve shirt and gloves. Fiberglass particles are very itchy when they get into your pores, so do what you can to avoid contact.
3. Sand the area around the ding with the 80-grit sandpaper.
4. If there's a hole in your foam, fill it will the filler-resin. Make sure you're working in a shady area; this stuff is specifically designed to dry rapidly in the sun. Now, place it in the sun to cure.
5. When the filler-resin is hard (this should only take about 5 to 15 minutes depending on how sunny it is and how big the ding is), sand it flush with the 120-grit sandpaper. It should sand pretty easily.
6. Cut the fiberglass cloth. Make sure the piece you cut completely covers the dinged area.
7. Place the cloth over the ding. Now (again, make sure you're in a shady spot), pour the resin (the *resin,* not the filler-resin) on the cloth. Make sure the cloth is completely saturated, including the edges, and that the resin is evenly applied. Use your fingers or an old credit card to help spread the resin. Stick the board in the sun to cure.
8. When the resin is dry (another 5 to 15 minutes), sand it with the 220-grit sandpaper until it is flush and smooth.
9. Board saved. Go surf.

QUICK FIX

If you're just dying to surf and don't have time to properly repair a ding, you can temporarily—*temporarily*—patch it by filling the puncture with wax or covering it with duct tape or a sticker. (Make sure to do the proper repairs as soon as you can.)

✦ YOUR FUTURE BOARD(S)

Eventually you'll reach a point in your surfing career where a shortboard may be a viable option for you. Some surfers choose to stick with a longboard or funboard, while others opt to venture into the ever-evolving world of shortboarding. Longboarding and shortboarding are two very different surfing species (see Chapter Four, "To Rip or Cruise?"). Once you're comfortable and confident on a longboard, experiment with a shortboard; you may find it better suits your style (or you may find that you never again want to be without your longboard). Either way, it's worth a try or a laugh.

Short *board*

A typical shortboard is usually about 6½ feet long, relatively narrow and thin, with a pointed nose, and nearly all shortboards are trifins. A shortboard is not as stable as a longboard, but for a more experienced surfer, its small size and pointed nose allow for much greater maneuverability (but far fewer mistakes). Choosing the right one will depend a lot on your height, weight, ability, and where you intend to surf. Discuss these factors with your more experienced friends, as well as the sales team at the various surf shops around town.

Fish

A fish is a short, flat, wide, stocky board built specifically for waves that are too small and slow to really enjoy with a standard shortboard. The beauty of the fish is that the width and flatness make it easier to catch smaller waves while the shorter length still allows for maneuverability. A fish is a wise buy for a seasoned shortboarder who wants to ride slop in the summer, but note: these boards stink in steeper, hollower waves.

Gun

Guns (or rhino chasers) are actually longer boards—7 plus feet—but are built for big-wave riding. Their narrow nose and tail allow for more control in bigger surf, and their length and volume make it possible to catch waves. Be aware of these boards. You don't want to mistakenly buy one for your first board. While they are big, like a hybrid or longboard, their pointed noses and tails make these boards less stable, and well, you'll just look silly, and nobody wants that. When you're physically and mentally ready to paddle into waves 12 feet and bigger, that's when you will need a gun.

✦ BOARD BREAKDOWN

As your surfing progresses, your equipment and the various subtleties between boards will become increasingly important—the series of numbers jotted down on the deck of your board will take on a whole new meaning. Surfers are very particular about their boards. In fact, many surfers have a stockpile of boards (called a *quiver;* from three to ten boards or more) to use for different conditions, breaks, even mood! There's the 6'5"with lots of rocker, the 7'2"pintail with the tapered rails, oh, and the 5'10" twinfin swallowtail fish. Ah, *what?*

Not to worry. Here's the translation:

Board *Dimensions*

Usually written somewhere on the deck of the board. The figures, measured in feet and inches, are usually noted in the following order: length/nose width/middle width/tail width/thickness. Occasionally you will see only the length/middle width/thickness. Note: Nose and tail width are measured 1 foot from each end of the board.

Rails

The edges of the surfboard. They range in thickness and shape and affect the board's turning ability. Your board's responsiveness when put on edge will be a top priority, especially if you choose to shortboard. If you're a first-time buyer, look for full, soft rails—they are the most forgiving.

Rocker

The curve of the board. Rocker impacts the board's speed as well as its ability to turn. More rocker slows the board down but shortens the board's turning radius, making it easier to carve quick turns. Most shortboarders hunt endlessly for a board with the perfect rocker: fast but agile.

Outline/Template

The outer shape of the board. It will tell you in general terms how the board will perform in the water. The straighter the outline, the faster the board, but the harder to turn; a more curved outline means less speed but easier turning.

Volume

The amount of foam used in a board. The more foam, the more buoyancy and stability. For beginners and heavier surfers, the board should have greater volume, while lighter or more experienced surfers require less volume.

Foil

The distribution of volume. Your board should be thickest underneath your chest and taper out evenly and smoothly toward the nose and tail.

Bottom

The underside of the surfboard (the part that is in contact with the water). The bottom affects the sensitivity of the board. Various types of bottom—vees, channels, concaves—increase sensitivity, but right now, a flatter or slightly convex bottom is your best bet.

Tail

The bottom end of the surfboard. It influences how your board will perform in varying types of surf. Some tails, like the narrow *pintail*, are designed for big, hollow surf, while others, such as the midwidth

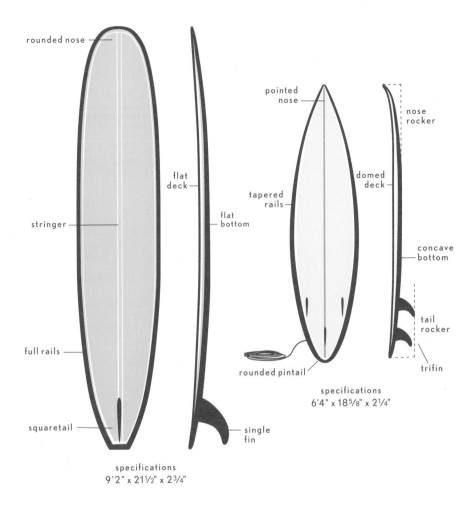

rounded nose

flat deck

stringer

flat bottom

full rails

squaretail

single fin

specifications
9'2" x 21½" x 2¾"

pointed nose

nose rocker

domed deck

tapered rails

concave bottom

tail rocker

trifin

rounded pintail

specifications
6'4" x 18⅝" x 2¼"

squaretail, are used in everyday boards for everyday conditions. You will see many different tail shapes out there, but really, they are all just some variation of the pintail or squaretail or a combination of both. A pintail is pointed, which allows a surfer to hold a line in larger, steeper surf. A squaretail is square(ish), giving it two pivot points (as opposed to the pintail's one), which makes it easier to turn. It also offers more surface area, which translates to increased buoyancy for those flat sections. The *squashtail* is a squaretail with soft corners; it performs essentially like a squaretail. A *roundtail* is an attempt to establish the perfect equilibrium between the pintail and the squaretail: buoyancy, release, and hold. And finally, the *swallowtail* looks like a squaretail with a V-shape cut into the board: the wider the V, the more like a squaretail; the narrower the V, the more like a pintail.

Deck

The top of the board, where you will stand and where you will put the wax (see "Wax," facing page). A domed deck is easier to put on edge and is seen most often on high-performance boards used in steeper, more powerful surf. The more buoyant flat deck, usually seen on boards designed for smaller, mushier waves, is less responsive, but more stable.

Stringer

A thin piece of wood (usually basswood or cedar) located in the middle of the board that runs from nose to tail. It affects the board's strength and flexibility. Some longboards and guns have three stringers for added strength and weight.

Fins

Gives forward drive and allows you to navigate and control the board. They are located on the back of the board at the tail. Fins come in a wide range of shapes, sizes, thicknesses, and materials that, some say, drastically change the feel and ride of your board. Thicker and/or larger fins provide more stability, while smaller and/or more flexible fins offer greater maneuverability. Most boards are shaped with either a one-, two-, or three-fin configuration in mind:

• **single fin:** One large, middle fin. Usually seen on classic longboards. Lots of drive, but not very responsive. Long turns. Some people swear by the ability of the single-fin design to hold traction in the tube.

• **twinfin:** Two midsized fins, one on either side of the board, near the tail. Twinfins are most often seen on small, wide-tailed boards; they tend to give you more speed, but have a much looser feel and can be hard to control. Twinfins were popular in the 1970s and early '80s, but are rarely seen today.

• **trifin:** Three fins, one fin in the middle, near the very end of the board, and two same-size or smaller fins on either side, a few inches forward of the rear fin. This is by far the most popular fin configuration because of its nice balance between stability and acceleration. Trifins are seen on virtually all shortboards and on about half of all longboards.

✦ ACCESSORIES

In addition to your board, there are certain accessories—wetsuits, hoods, booties, trunks, flip-flops, and hats—that can add to your comfort and style. It is important to remember, however, that all you *really* need to surf is a board and a wave. Do not get overwhelmed by the laundry list of gear seen in this chapter—it's just a guide. You are the one who decides what are musts and what are maybes.

Leash

A leash is a long plastic cord that attaches you to your board (it should run about the length of your board). At one end of the cord there is a Velcro strap that fits around your ankle, and at the other end is a string that ties to a special plug built into the tail of your board. Make sure the string does not extend over the rail or it may cut into your board. Each end of the leash should also be equipped with a swivel so that the cord doesn't get kinked and twisted (*never* buy a leash without a double swivel).

In the beginning, always use a leash! You do not want your board getting away from you; not only is it a pain (and tiring) to swim after it, a free board can be dangerous to you and the surfers around you.

Wax

Before you head out into the big, bad surf, you need to wax the deck of your board. Wax provides the all-important traction between your feet and your board. If your board is new, you'll want to first put on a layer of base coat wax and then apply a second layer of regular wax, which is much softer. Note: After you've put on the initial layer of base coat and layer of wax, any subsequent surf sessions will only require a fresh coat of *regular* wax.

Different types of wax are appropriate for different temperatures of water. Make sure you use the right type of wax for the water temperature where you'll be surfing. Here's a general categorization of what type of wax you'll need for certain water temperatures:

• Cold water wax: below 58°F
• Cool water wax: 58° to 68°F
• Warm water wax: 68° to 78°F
• Tropical water wax: over 78°F

Each brand varies slightly in terms of the appropriate temperature range, so double-check the label before you buy it.

application: When applying the base coat and wax, be generous, and make sure you hit all of the areas where your body will be in contact with the board. On the first application (if you have a longboard), use almost an entire bar of base coat, and then follow it up with close to an entire bar of wax (remember, on future applications, you'll need only a thin layer of wax to maintain a sticky, adhesive deck). Rub on the wax in a circular motion, without pressing down too hard, so that small bumps are formed—you're creating a nonskid surface. Once your board is waxed, it's primed to hit the waves.

cleaning: From time to time you may want to clean your board. This means scraping off all of the old layers of wax and then reapplying a fresh coat. Leave your board in the sun for a few minutes to soften the wax; this will make it much easier to clean. Use the straight edge of a wax comb, a specially designed tool available at surf shops, to clear off the wax (an ice scraper, old credit card, or a cassette tape case also work well). Or if you let the wax get really hot, you can use sand to scrub it off. Once your board is completely clean, take it out of the sun, let it cool, and then apply a fresh base coat followed by fresh layer of regular wax just as you did when the board was new.

Traction Pads

These rubber pads are usually seen on shortboards. They adhere to the rear deck of the board and provide better, you guessed it, *traction* for the back foot. Some surfers swear by them, but others find that the pads tear up their knees or that they simply prefer the feel of wax.

Board Bags

daily protection: For daily travel and protection, some surfers keep their boards in either a terrycloth sock or a lightweight plastic case. Both the sock and the case provide great UV protection and help prevent yellowing and breakdown of the fiberglass. However, as anyone who has ever put on or taken off a board sock will attest, it's a royal pain—think of pantyhose and a wet leg—and if the board gets too hot, the wax has a tendency to melt into the sock.

My advice: Go with the case. Though they are a little more expensive, they offer a bit more protection than the sock, they are easier to keep clean, and you can put the board in and take the board out with much more ease. Bonus: Cases have handles and usually come with a shoulder strap, which makes carrying your board, especially a longboard, slightly less cumbersome. Of course, if you can't afford a case, a sock is better than nothing.

travel protection: If you're traveling with your board, especially on an airplane, you'll need a travel bag. You can find them at any surf shop. A travel bag is heavily padded and will protect your board from getting damaged. Some bags (usually called *coffins*) are big enough to fit more than one board. If you plan to take multiple boards, make sure you individually wrap each one in a towel or bubble wrap before you put them in the bag. And always remember to remove the fins before you pack the boards. If your fins are glassed on, make sure you wrap them thoroughly. (For more board-packing tips see, "Packing Your Board," page 129.)

FREEWHEELING

Unless you have your own personal Sherpa, lugging a board bag around stuffed with three boards is taxing to put it mildly. There are, however, bags available with wheels—find them, buy them; your back and shoulders will be grateful!

✦ WETSUITS

Wetsuits are neoprene suits that keep you toasty in cooler water. They insulate your body, reducing the loss of body heat, which allows you to stay in the water longer. Wetsuits range in design from a simple vest (sleeveless, top-only suit) to a spring suit (short sleeves and legs) to a full suit (long arms, long legs), and come in a dizzying array of styles and sizes made just for women. Today's wetsuits are lightweight and flexible, but do restrict movement somewhat (the thicker the wetsuit, the more restrictive) making paddling—or any movement for that matter—a little tougher. This is an unfortunate reality of surfing in a wetsuit, but take heart, it does get easier and more comfortable as your body adjusts to the suit. Just give it some time.

This lucky girl will be surfing
in water 73°F and above.

She's dressed for braving
water between 50° and 55°F.

Size Breakdown

The pendulum on this swings pretty wide. The size that will fit you could vary depending on the brand of wetsuit. Usually wetsuit makers provide size charts that most surf shops post on the wall near the wetsuits. Use these charts as an initial guide and ask someone for help.

THE BIG SQUEEZE

Keep in mind that until you're used to your wetsuit it will undoubtedly feel uncomfortably snug and will be hard to put on and take off. Don't worry, you'll get the hang of it.

Thickness Breakdown

Wetsuits come in a range of thickness combinations. The most common is the 3/2 (3 mm thick in the torso, 2 mm thick in the arms and legs), but there are thinner and thicker suits available depending on your need. See the temperature/thickness guide below for help.

73°F+	Vest, rash guard (see page 52)
65° to 72°F	2/1 or 2/2 spring suit
55° to 65°F	3/2 full suit
50° to 55° F	4/3 full suit + gloves, booties, and hood
40° to 50°F	5/3 full suit + gloves, booties, and hood
40°F and below!	Dry suit (completely waterproof) + gloves, booties, and hood

Shop•talk:

When referring to a 3/2 wetsuit say, "a *three two*." Likewise, when you're referring to a 4/3 say, "a *four three*." The same goes for a 2/1, or "*two one*." Get the idea?

To Zip or Not to Zip

Debatable. Some people prefer a wetsuit with a zipper (easier in-out access), while others swear by the no-zip variety (slightly more flexible). It's really up to you. Pick the one that fits the best and the one that you can manage to put on single-handedly—remember, you won't have the sales lady around for help when you're standing half-naked outside your car in the freezing cold trying to wiggle into or out of your blasted wetsuit.

Wetsuit Shopping Tips

• When it comes to wetsuits, you pretty much get what you pay for, so if you surf a lot, this may be one time you actually want to throw down the cash for the best suit you can find.

• Try on a bunch of styles, brands, and sizes—they all fit differently—until you find just the right cut. Be strategic; be thorough; stay focused.

• Check the seams. Make sure they are carefully and securely glued, sewn, or taped. The stronger the seams, the warmer you'll be, and the longer your wetsuit will last.

• Make sure your suit is snug but not immobilizing. Don't be afraid to walk around the shop, do a couple knee bends, a karate chop or two, a few arm circles. Make sure you have full range of motion and freedom of movement.

• Ask a sales person to double-check that you've found the right fit. And if you don't feel comfortable having a perfect stranger give you a thorough once-over, bring a wetsuit-savvy friend along.

• Oh, and do not undertake this sometimes-arduous task on a hot day: sheer agony.

Wetsuit Longevity

Unfortunately, neoprene does wear out, so over the years, you'll need to occasionally replace your existing suit with a new one. If you surf a lot and live where the water temperature requires you to wear a wetsuit year-round (you're a dedicated, admirable soul and deserve huge kudos!), your suit will probably only last you a little over a year. But if you're more of a fair-weather surfer (that's okay—there are a lot of us) and your wetsuit doesn't get much use, it could last you up to four years.

Wetsuit TLC

Your wetsuit deserves the same love and attention as your surfboard. When you get home from surfing, *do not* leave your wetsuit in your car—ah, the stench! Instead, take a few minutes to rinse it out with fresh water and let it air dry. (*Absolutely do not put your wetsuit in the washer or dryer*—certain wetsuit death.) Routine rinsing and air-drying will not only help prolong your wetsuit's lifespan, but will keep you from having to put on a cold, wet, smelly, moldy wetsuit the next time you go surfing—not pleasant. When air drying, avoid using a hanger; over time this tends to weaken the shoulder seams. And you may also want to invest in a wetsuit repair kit for any tears or failing seams that occur.

TINKLE TIME

There will come a time when you're surfing in a wetsuit and you have to pee. You could hold it and be completely miserable, or you could just go, right there, in your wetsuit. To the uninitiated this may seem rather foul, but it's true: Most surfers would rather pee in their wetsuits than cut short a perfectly good surf session to go to the bathroom.

Removing a wetsuit can be a bit of a challenge. Though there will always be some unavoidable wiggling and pulling involved, your best exit strategy (for you and for the longevity of your wetsuit—too many hard jerks and tugs can be tough on the seams) is to roll the wetsuit off your body—first shoulders, then arms, torso, and legs. At the last stage, when the wetsuit is down around your ankles and you're trying to free your feet, hold onto your car, a wall, a pole, anything stable and stationary, to avoid hopping about, losing your balance, and toppling over.

Booties

Booties are rubber-soled, neoprene socks that are worn in cold water. They can also be used at reef or rock breaks to prevent cuts, or at well-known sea urchin haunts to avoid punctures (this particular type of bootie is usually called a *reef walker* and cuts off just below the ankle as opposed to the cold water bootie, which cuts off a few inches above the ankle). Many people don't mind wearing booties; in addition to protection, they also provide great traction on your board. But some surfers feel they are less responsive to the board when wearing booties and opt for bare feet regardless of the water temperature or conditions. It's up to you.

Gloves

Neoprene gloves are a great choice for someone surfing in very cold water. Again, to wear or not to wear gloves is a personal preference. Depending on your cold tolerance, you may not need them.

Hoods

You may look like one of the lesser superheroes, and you may feel like a cannonball, but wearing a hood drastically reduces heat loss from your head and will keep you much warmer in cold water. It's definitely worth a try if you frequently surf in waters below 60°F and have no problem swallowing your pride.

Rash Guards

Rash guards are thin Lycra or neoprene water shirts that provide protection from the sun and wind, and prevent skin abrasions on your chest caused by hours spent paddling on your surfboard. (Some people also wear them under their wetsuits to add another layer of insulation.) They come with short sleeves or long sleeves, and in a variety of colors. Important note: If you are going to spend any time surfing in the blazing sun of the tropics, invest in a rash guard! It offers the maximum protection from the sun, and you will undoubtedly need it.

Bikinis

There is a difference between a sunning bikini and a surfing bikini. Sunning bikinis tend to be small and flimsy—perfect for hanging out on the beach but not such a wise choice for surfing. Surfing bikinis are still sexy but are more durable, offer a bit more coverage, and tend to stay put. When looking for a surfing suit, try on a bunch of styles. Look for the cut that best suits your body type and that you are the most comfortable wearing. Make sure you're not going to pop out the second you hit the water; the *last thing* you want to be caught doing when a huge wave is rolling toward you is readjusting your suit.

Trunks/Board Shorts

Trunks are durable shorts that are designed for surfing. They have no open pockets so you don't drag water as you paddle and they dry exceptionally fast. If you don't mind the funky tan line, trunks are a great addition to your surfing accoutrement, especially if you're a little self-conscious about parading around in your swimsuit. And they also eliminate the imminent threat of the bum-revealing wedgie that comes with wearing a bikini bottom when you surf. If you have a hard time finding something in the women's section, check out the men's trunks—a size 31 usually fits a women's size 6. Men's trunks tend to come in more subdued colors (let's face it, we don't all like to wear pink and baby blue) and are usually a bit longer and sometimes more flattering.

Flip-*Flops*

Flip-flops, also known as thongs or slaps, are a must-have if you're going to spend any significant time at the beach (honestly, every surfer owns at least two pairs). They're easy on, easy off, inexpensive, easy to hide, and most importantly, you can wear them with wet or sandy feet. No, you can't go jogging in them, and if you're planning to walk any long distances, you'll probably want something more supportive, but for beachside play, it's the only way to go.

SPF

To state the obvious: Sunscreen is very important, especially when you're in the water where there is no shelter from the sun. Lube up at least ten minutes before you hit the waves so the lotion has time to absorb, and make sure the sunscreen you use is waterproof and sweatproof. If you're spending a lot of time in the water, reapply your sunscreen religiously. Keep a tube in your car or beach bag at all times so you are never without it. And don't forget the often-overlooked lips and ears.

zinc: For total sun blockage, use zinc oxide. It's great for prominent features like the nose, cheeks, and lips that absorb a lot of sun (or if you need to protect a scar). And you no longer have to look like you're wearing tribal face paint; many companies offer tinted zinc that blends in with most skin colors, so you can barely tell it's on.

hats: For extra sun protection, you can wear a hat when surfing small waves, but don't be disappointed if (*when*) it gets washed off and

BELEN KIMBLE-CONNELLY: "Ella Bache SPF 30 (from Australia) *DOES NOT COME OFF AT ALL.* Or Dermalogica SPF 30 body spray."

MARY OSBORNE: "Shiseido. You can buy it in any department store. It's a stick and almost looks like makeup when it's on . . . in tropical places, *I LIVE BY IT!*"

CARLA ROWLAND: "I like pretty much anything made for babies— *IT USUALLY DOESN'T RUN IN MY EYES.*"

PAULINE MENCZER: "The strongest stuff I can find. I'm not that fussy."

SERENA BROOKE: "I use Sol Sunguard and La Roche SPF 60—*ITS GOT A LOT OF ZINC IN IT.*"

disappears in the whitewater. You can buy a hat specifically designed for surfing (they're usually waterproof and have a strap that secures under your chin) if you don't mind forgoing fashion for function.

The Surf Mobile

Now that you've got the gear, you'll need the appropriate transport to the beach. Here are a few suggestions on how to transform your urban battlewagon into a fully equipped surf mobile.

racks: Unless you have a truck or a station wagon big enough to hold your surfboard, you'll need to buy a surfboard rack for the roof of your car. You can choose between a soft rack and a permanent rack. Soft racks can be taken on and off with relative ease. They are not as sturdy as permanent racks, but they are safe and work well (and can be used on rental cars when you take surf trips!). Permanent racks attach (actually lock) to the roof of your car. People who surf a lot tend to buy permanent racks so they don't have to deal with the putting on and taking off of the rack every time they want to surf. If you plan to surf a few times a week, invest in a permanent rack—it will make your life much easier. But if you're an on-again, off-again surfer, a soft rack should do the trick.

securing your board on the rack: When you put your board on the rack, make sure you place the deck facedown and the fins in the front. This makes for a bit of wind resistance, but it keeps your board from sliding out of the straps (and also signals to the surfing world you are not a rookie). Tightly strap the board down and be sure to tuck in any loose ends or they will flap around and make really irritating noises. A word of caution: Once you've thrown your board up on the rack, don't forget to *actually* strap it down before you tear off down the road.

BOARD PILEUP

If you're putting more than one board on your rack, make sure to stack them in order of size with the largest on the bottom—facedown, fins forward, of course. Put a towel between each board (if they are not already in a board bag) and place the tail of each board inside the fins of the board that precedes it.

tunes: You will, of course, need the appropriate motivational music to accompany you on your way to the beach, so make sure you always have your favorite tunes cued up before you hit the road.

Every surf mobile must be equipped with a surf coffer: a plastic box and lid (I suggest Rubbermaid) that contains everything you could possibly need to make your surfing experience the greatest it can be. (And no, perfectly peeling, chest-high waves are not included.)

Here's what to store inside:

+ Rash guard
+ Extra leash and leash string
+ Fin key
+ Wax (keep this in a zippered plastic bag—wax has an uncanny tendency to get all over everything!)
+ Base coat
+ Wax comb/ice scraper/tape case/old credit card
+ Duct tape
+ Towel
+ Sunscreen
+ Zinc
+ Visor or sun hat
+ Warm beanie for cooler days
+ Sweatshirt
+ Brush/comb
+ Hair band/barrette
+ Saline (if you wear contacts)
+ Bottle of water
+ First-aid kit
+ Tampons
+ Gallon jug of fresh water for post-surf body and feet rinsing
+ Booties
+ Extra plastic container to transport wet wetsuit

You can find first-aid kits at most drugstores, or your local Red Cross chapter. Or you can build your own.

A good kit contains (but is certainly not limited to) the following goodies:

+ Adhesive tape
+ Antibiotic ointment
+ Antiseptic towelettes
+ Bandages
+ Hand soap
+ Heat-reflective emergency/survival cover
+ Hydrogen peroxide
+ Cold pack
+ Disposable gloves
+ Gauze pads or roller gauze
+ Insect sting–relief medicated pads
+ Meat tenderizer
+ Plastic bags
+ Rubbing alcohol
+ Scissors
+ Tweezers with magnifying glass
+ Small flashlight and batteries
+ Triangular bandage with two safety pins

Chapter 3:
The Fundamentals

✦ THE POP-UP:
IT'S A SNAP

Your surfing career doesn't actually start in the water. It can and should begin at home. Yes, your living room floor (or front yard or wherever you have enough room to spread yourself out) is the perfect spot to learn how to pop up from the prone to standing position, as you will do when you've caught a wave. It is important to practice the pop-up on solid, stable ground before you try it on a fast-moving surfboard (on a fast-moving wave). Once you feel confident and comfortable with your popping-up abilities on land, it's time to take them to the water.

The Dry Run

The pop-up should be done in one, smooth, fluid, quick motion. Think *paddle, paddle, paddle, bang*—you're up. Start by lying down on your stomach, with your hands, palms down, on either side of your chest, and legs together. Now, as quickly as you can and in one movement, push yourself up and away from the floor, arching your back, as you simultaneously pull your feet and legs underneath you. You should end up in a crouched position, head up and eyes looking forward, feet slightly wider than your shoulders, relaxed, bent knees, hips low, chest up, with one foot in front of the other, back foot perpendicular to what would be the length of your board, front foot turned out ever so slightly; arms are just bent and out from your sides, slightly forward. As you are going through the motions, say to yourself: snap. Try it again; snap. And again; snap. Snap. Be fast, be smooth, be explosive. Practice this until you're able to do it with grace, speed, and consistency.

1. Palm down, legs together.

2. Snap!

3. Think speed. Think
fluidity. Think grace.

4. Head and chest up,
eyes forward, hips low,
knees bent—charge!

Do yourself a favor: Every morning after your coffee and before your shower, do ten sets of pop-ups. With just a little bit of dedication, this movement will quickly become second nature.

You will notice that you have a natural tendency to put either your left or right foot forward. Go with it. Our bodies know what works for us and what feels comfortable; there's no right or wrong forward foot. In fact, there are names for both. If you put your left foot forward, you're a regularfoot, and if you put your right foot forward, you're a goofyfoot. (And there should be no negative connotation here—you're goofy in a good way!)

+ Rochelle Ballard: regular
+ Serena Brooke: regular
+ Heather Clark: goofy
+ Julie Cox: regular
+ Kim Hamrock: goofy
+ Margeaux Hamrock: regular
+ Belen Kimble-Connelly: regular
+ Pauline Menczer: regular
+ Mary Osborne: regular
+ Carla Rowland: goofy who goes switchfoot
+ Frieda Zamba: goofy

✦ CHARGING THE SURF ZONE

Leash Lessons

Resist the urge to put on your leash until you are on the beach and ready to enter the water. Do this for two reasons: As you walk from your car to the beach, you don't want to trip over the leash, fall, and hurt (or make a spectacle of) yourself, nor do you want to been seen by other surfers as the oblivious rookie roaming around town strapped to your board. Before you attach your leash, first pull it taunt to remove any twists or kinks, and then secure it to what will be your back ankle (right ankle for regularfoots, left for goofyfoots) with the cord positioned on the outside of your ankle. This will keep the leash from getting tangled up in your legs while you're surfing, which can be really embarrassing and dangerous. Once you've put on your leash but before you sprint into the water, don't forget to hold the slack of your leash so you don't trip; save your wipeouts for the water. Finally, when your surf session is over, remove your leash and wrap it around the tail of your board before you charge off to the car.

PRE-SURF YOGA

It's a good idea to do a little stretching before you surf. Pick up a good yoga book for some stretching ideas. In fact, yoga is not only a fantastic way to stretch before you surf, it is also the perfect cross-training exercise for surfers. Beyond stretching, you'll improve your strength, your flexibility, your balance, and your focus. If you can't motivate to set up a home ashram, try a class.

Paddling

Paddling is 50 percent of surfing. It gets you out to the lineup, it gets you into the right position, it gets you into the wave, and it gets you out of danger. Learning how to paddle efficiently is crucial to your overall surfing performance and safety. When you first start surfing, paddling can be a serious workout. It not only requires a certain level of skill, it also demands a certain amount of back and arm strength that some of us have yet to build. Not to worry, with some training and practice, you and your muscles will get there. The bottom line: The more you surf, the stronger and better your paddling will become, so get out there as often as you can. Even if you're not riding waves, go out and just paddle around. Get comfortable on your board. Get familiar with how the correct body position feels and then spend some time simply practicing your stroke.

The Stroke

Paddling is essentially swimming the crawl stroke, but you're on a surfboard. So like the crawl, your arms are alternating: one arm pulls while the other arm reaches forward. As you pull the water make sure your hand mimics the shape of an arc, moving from the outside in toward the center of the board and then out again. Cup your hands slightly (keyword: *slightly*), which will help you pull more water with each stroke, increasing your speed. And as you stroke, keep your elbows bent—remember, your paddle should resemble a modified freestyle.

CROSS TRAINING

Open-ocean swimming is a great way to train, as is logging time in a pool. Make sure you mix it up and include both endurance and sprint swims. Other cross-training ideas include underwater sprinting, running, aerobics/dancing, yoga, Pilates, beach volleyball, jumping rope, hiking, in-line skating, and mountain biking.

66 Stretch for any size surf as a daily regime to keep you loose and flexible. Always paddle hard no matter what size the waves are—this will keep you in shape for when the swell comes up. OCEAN SWIMMING AND BODY SURFING ARE ALSO EXTREMELY HELPFUL. I LIKE TO HOLD MY BREATH BODY SURFING TO LEARN BREATH CONTROL . . . [To train] for more extreme surf I run in thick, heavy sand for at least a couple of miles with sprints. [During the sprints] I will hold my breath for as long as I can. (This is for the two-wave hold down!) . . . Jumping rope for up to a half hour helps your stamina. Martial arts is also an excellent form of cross training both mentally and physically. Oh yeah, I also like to play with a 14-pound medicine ball! Catch anyone? **99**

Beyond Stroke: *Paddling Pointers*

Technique is an important part of paddling and will work wonders on your paddling efficiency. Here are a few tips that should help take some of the pain out of your paddling:

• **head up:** Keep your head up so you can see exactly where you are going and what is happening around you.

• **legs together:** Keep your legs together. This helps to stabilize the board, allowing it to more easily glide through the water as well as reduce drag.

stall: bad

pearl: bad

centered: good

• **body centered:** A level board is a fast board. Make sure you are balanced and centered on your board. (If you weren't keeping your head up, your chin would rest about a quarter of the way down from the top of the board.) When you're in the right spot—you'll be able to feel it, and it feels good!—your board will easily glide across the water. When you're in the wrong spot, which will also be glaringly obvious to you, several things can happen. If your weight is too far forward on your board, the board will *pearl*, or nose-dive into the water, making it nearly impossible to move—anywhere. If your weight is too far back, the nose of your board will pop up, and you will *stall*, literally. If it's too far to the right or left, the corresponding rail will submerge, which will also slow you down. Stay centered and stable. Try not to rock back and forth (your arms should really be the only thing moving), and keep the nose of the board about 2 inches above the water.

ON YOUR KNEES

Though not a terribly efficient way to paddle, knee paddling uses different muscle groups than the traditional prone paddle, which can be a nice reprieve for tired muscles. It allows you a higher vantage point from which to spy incoming waves, and it can also earn you some old-school style points. It does require a certain degree of balance, but with some practice, you'll get it. Sit down on your knees in the middle of your board. Adjust your body weight until you feel balanced and stable. Bend over slightly and pull the water with your forearms. Your arms should be working in unison, not alternating. At least for now, only use the knee paddle for short distances, and be aware that, on some boards, knee paddling can create pressure dings. Also note: This paddling technique can only be done on a longboard.

Riding the Whitewater

Before staking your claim in the lineup (the area where surfers sit and wait for waves), you should first practice—and master—the basics in the whitewater. Some beginning surfers ride whitewater for days, even weeks, before moving on to unbroken waves. It's not as glamorous or as fun as catching a bona fide wave, but it's the best place to get familiar with your board, get comfortable in the water, and nurture some confidence. Once you get the hang of catching and riding the whitewater and get better at controlling your board, you can head for the lineup. Until then, stick with the soup.

Position yourself far enough from shore so that you have plenty of room to catch and ride the whitewater without hitting the beach, but not so far out that you will be in the way of surfers who are riding the set waves. You may want to first wade out past the immediate shorebreak before jumping on your board to paddle. As you wade, keep your board to your side (nose pointed at the wave)—you don't want it to come between you and a wave—and lift the nose up over any incoming waves. Once you're a reasonable distance from shore, you can climb atop your board and practice your paddling.

Julie Cox on sticking with it:

66 YES, I'VE WANTED TO QUIT SURFING . . . A FEW TIMES. One time was when I was first starting and I was so frustrated. I hit a rough patch and wasn't improving as fast as I wanted. BUT I COULDN'T BRING MYSELF TO GIVE IT UP; I loved the feel of the water, the CHALLENGE each day of surfing brought, and the community I was becoming involved with. Recently I had to take a break from surfing due to an injury and I thought maybe this was a sign that I should sell my boards and get more serious about a career, BUT I WAS OVER THAT PRETTY QUICKLY! **99**

soup master

Your **First Ride**

When the whitewater of an already broken wave comes rushing toward you, turn yourself around to face the shore and lie down on your board. Make sure you are centered and stable, the board is level, and you are perpendicular to the incoming wave. Now, you're ready to roll. Paddle like you've never paddled before. Really put some muscle into it. Continue to paddle until you feel the momentum of the whitewater take hold (this is an unequivocal feeling)—do not stop paddling until you do. Once you're sure you've caught the whitewater and feel stable on your board, pop up (*snap!*) to your feet as you practiced in your living room. Remember: no knees! Stabilize yourself, feet slightly wider than your shoulders, knees just bent, hips low, chest up, one foot in front of the other, back foot perpendicular to your board, front foot turned out slightly—wahoo! You're surfing!

Do this over and over and over again. It may take you a while to get the hang of it, but you will. And when you do, it's time to take it to the next level: the lineup.

Frieda Zamba on her first ride:

❝ I was twelve and it was summertime at my beach, Flagler Beach. I remember being so happy that it was summer and school was out, but I also remember being very bored and wanting to do something

DIFFERENT THAT SUMMER. I was sitting on the sand watching all my friends—boys—surf, thinking that it looked kind of fun, but I didn't have a board. I noticed this girl come down to the beach with a really cool blue board. She paddled out and just sat there and could barely ride the waves . . . Immediately I ran down to the water and motioned to her to come in. SHE CAME IN AND I ASKED HER IF I COULD TRY SURFING. SHE LAUGHED AND SAID GIVE IT A GO . . . I always watched the boys do it and kind of [had an] idea of what you're supposed to do. [When] I got far enough out from the beach I turned around and [pointed] the board toward shore. All of a sudden I felt this burst of water push me forward with so much

POWER I COULD BARELY HANG ON. Then I thought *this is just like doing a push-up, but you just keep coming up,* and I was on my feet suddenly. I felt small and the ocean seemed so big and powerful. The board felt like I was riding a chunk of cork; it would move at the slightest movement I made.

IT WAS THE COOLEST THING I HAD EVER FELT . . . AND I KNEW I WANTED TO FEEL LIKE THAT AS MUCH AS POSSIBLE. [And] let's just say the expression on the girl's face when she saw me riding was pure shock. She put an end to my wave riding real quick by grabbing her board and saying, 'You just got lucky.' The rest of the summer I spent mowing lawns so I could save up to buy [my own] board. **❞**

The Art *of* Wiping Out

Wipeouts are inevitable. We all do it and will continue to do it for the rest of our surfing careers. There is, however, a right and wrong way to wipe out. Let's focus on the right way to do it. When you fall, first and foremost, fall seaward, away from your board (this will help you avoid being drilled by the lip of the wave or your board), and cover your head (you never want to leave your head unprotected and vulnerable). Be cognizant of how deep or shallow the water is and the type of bottom—sand, rock, reef—and try to fall appropriately; for shallow water, fall flat; for a reef or rock bottom, don't wildly kick your feet or stand up. And finally, just relax. Fighting the water will use up your energy and oxygen. Just let go and let the wave pass. When it has officially rolled by and the waters have settled, that's when it's time to follow your bubbles (or your leash) to the surface.

Mary Osborne on wiping out:

66 WHEN I WAS LEARNING HOW TO SURF I PEARLED SO BADLY THE BOARD CAME BACK AND HIT ME RIGHT IN THE NOSE. Blood was gushing out of my nostrils and I thought for sure I broke my nose. (I didn't.) I went in and got fixed up by my neighbor and was back in the water in an hour. YOU'VE JUST GOT TO KEEP GOING. 99

Belen Kimble-Connelly on her worst wipeout:

66 SUNSET LAST YEAR. When I paddled out it was only about 5 feet max, but I had not called the buoy report to see if the swell was picking up. So I am out there and it just keeps getting bigger and bigger, slowly from 6 to 7 feet, then 8 to 10 feet. THEN OUT OF NOWHERE COMES A SOLID 15-FOOT SET. I was caught inside and there was no way that I could have paddled out fast enough to get outside, and no way that I could get my board through those waves; my only option was to turn around and try to get the first wave. I turned around, took off, free fell down the face, and took the lip on the head. The wave pushed me down so deep that it was black. I had no idea which way was up or down. My vest came over my head and broke my leash. My board was taken all the way to shore. When I finally came up I had to take a quick breath before another huge set landed on my head. Luckily I stayed calm and relaxed. It took me about twenty minutes to swim in. When I got to shore I threw up and started crying. It was heavy and really shook me up, but it didn't stop me from getting back in the water. IT DID TEACH ME TO PAY MORE ATTENTION TO THE WAVES AND WHAT'S GOING ON WITH THE OCEAN, and to just stay calm because that is what will help you out the most. 99

Paddling *out to the* Lineup

Paddling out to the lineup can be a little dicey. Before you paddle out, make sure the waves are the appropriate size for your ability. Occasionally the swell can be big and consistent, which gives you little time to rest between sets. Once you're in surfing shape and feel comfortable out there, this may be just fine with you. But if you're still learning, conquering smaller waves that come with slightly less frequency is your best bet. (If when paddling out you continue to get pummeled, it's probably not the day for you, nor is it much fun. Ride the whitewater to shore and go somewhere else, or give it another try tomorrow.) Before you head out, spend at least ten minutes on the beach watching the waves and the other surfers. Be aware of how they are making it out to the lineup—this is most likely the path of least resistance—and then follow suit. Wait until there is a lull between sets and then sprint for it. Once you've started to paddle out, don't stop to wipe your hair out of your eyes or adjust your swimsuit or chitchat with a friend—that's just enough time for a set to roll in and wash you back to shore. Save that stuff for when you're safely beyond the breaking waves.

A WORD TO THE WINDED

Paddling can be extremely tiring, especially if the surf is consistent, meaning the sets are rolling in close together. Always remember that if you're too tired to paddle, you're probably too tired to surf safely. When your arms feel like mush, it's time to call it a day.

FREE RIDE

Channels are areas of deep water where waves don't usually break and are great spots to paddle out. Certain mild rip currents can also make paddling out a breeze, but should be used with extreme caution (for more information see "Rip Currents," page 114).

The lineup can be more than a little intimidating. Just take a deep breath and go for it. There's a rightful spot for anyone who wants to surf (or learn how to surf—we were all beginners once). A word of caution, however: There will be some days when the lineup is sparse, and some days when it is packed with hungry, aggressive surfers. If you're just starting to surf, give yourself a little room for error, and go out on days when it's not crowded. (See Chapter Five for more about etiquette and safety.)

Dealing with lineup machismo:

KIM HAMROCK: "After years of hassles and fights (part of the Danger Woman nickname) I have found the best way to deal with this is to just SMILE AND SURF! Let your surfing do the talking. Remember there are a lot more nice guys than there are mean ones. As long as you know the rules and surf in waves fit to your ability, most guys do not mind women in the lineup."

MARY OSBORNE: "Some people are jerks, but some people may live at that spot or have surfed for longer than you, so just be nice and deal with it. The more water time you have, the better you will become, and eventually people will start respecting you."

CARLA ROWLAND: "If you can surf and guys are hassling you, stuff 'em. If you are a beginner, JUST TRY TO STAY OUT OF THEIR WAY and maybe tell them to chill out."

Wading Out

To save yourself some energy, you may want to wade out past the shorebreak (just as you did in the whitewater) before you jump on your board and begin paddling. Remember, keep your board to your side and lift the nose up over any incoming waves.

Punch Through

If the waves are small enough, you can simply punch through them while paddling. As a breaking wave rushes toward you, paddle, paddle, paddle as hard as you can—don't stop paddling. Just before the wave hits, put your head down, grab the rails of your board tightly, and meet it straight on. Make sure the board is pointed directly into the wave, this will help lower the board's resistance to the wave. The wave will push you back slightly, but it won't wash you off your board.

Push-Up

The push-up is a modified version of punching through a wave and should be used only in small waves. Again, paddle straight toward the wave, but this time, when the wave is about to hit, push yourself up and let the water rush past in the space between your board and your body. When the wave has rolled by, lie back down on your board, get centered and stable, and start paddling again.

punch through

Turtle *Roll*

The turtle roll is a technique used by most longboarders. It's very effective but can be a little scary if you've never done it before. Don't be afraid: It's over in seconds, and actually, once you get the hang of it, it feels routine. As a wave approaches, grab onto the rails of the board with your hands, holding your body very close (and parallel) to the board. Quickly flip the board over (yes, you will momentarily be underwater), fin side up, continue to press your body against the board, and let the wave roll over you. Make sure the board is pointing directly into the wave. Once the wave has passed, flip back over, adjust your position, and begin paddling again, simple as that.

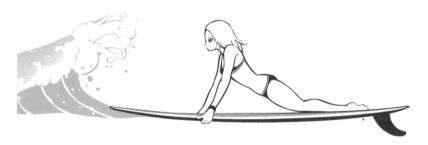

push-up

turtle roll

66 Most importantly KEEP YOUR ELBOWS SLIGHTLY BENT in so that they PROTECT you if the force of the wave pushes your board into you ... HAVE A DEATH GRIP ON THE RAILS OF THE BOARD! Depending on the wave, I will either press the board tightly against me or have it separated from my body shoving the board toward the top of the wave (this is the method I use the most). Wait for the PRESSURE OF THE WAVE to release you, flip the board back over, and keep paddling. I do not grip the board with my legs—if the board slips you can easily cut your legs on the fins. **99**

Duck-Dive

The duck-dive is pretty much the exclusive domain of the shortboarders. (Most longboards are way too big and buoyant to duck-dive successfully.) When duck-diving, you, along with your board, dive under the wave. It can be difficult to learn, but once you get the hang of it, it comes in really handy when you're surfing in bigger waves (see "To Rip: Shortboarding Basics," page 94, for how to duck-dive).

Bail Out

Worst-case scenario: You get caught off guard by a set of waves that are too big for a punch through, push-up, turtle roll, or duck-dive. When this happens, you should ditch your board and dive under the wave, in other words: bail out. There are several precautions you need to take before ditching your board. First and foremost, make sure no one is behind you—you don't want your board clobbering some poor, innocent soul who is also fighting to get outside. Second, if at all possible, try to position your board so that it is parallel (not perpendicular) to the breaking wave; this will allow the board to harmoniously roll with the wave rather than fight against it, which will reduce the risk that your board will be snapped. When the wave has passed, use your leash to find and collect your board, hop back on, and paddle like mad for the horizon.

Shop•talk:

If you find yourself constantly battling the whitewater as you make your way out to the lineup, most likely a set has rolled in and you are what is called caught *inside*—not fun, but a common occurrence. Once you paddle beyond the breaking waves, you can rest comfortably (thankfully) on the *outside*.

✦ BONA FIDE SURFING

Waves are fickle and hard to read, and catching them is not as easy as it seems. In fact, it may take a few sessions before you find yourself in just the right place at just the right time. That's okay. Don't get frustrated. Even the best surfers miss perfectly good waves. Get used to it.

Wave selection:

CARLA ROWLAND: "Always look for a WORKABLE SHOULDER. Don't just go for the sake of going. The first wave in the set is not always the best one."

SERENA BROOKE: "Look for a wave that's COMING IN AT AN ANGLE, where it's not breaking ahead of itself down the line. You want a wave that is not super steep down the line because then it's going to close out on you."

JULIE COX: "In contests you always want to try to catch the bigger waves that will give you A LONG RIDE. But in free surfing, I just catch whatever will break. I'm not picky!"

When you're out in the lineup and you hear someone yell *"Outside!"* this means a big set has been spotted. Paddle like mad for the horizon. You don't want to get caught in front of an enormous breaking wave— no fun.

The **Waiting** Game

You will spend a good portion of your time in the water waiting for a wave. All surfers play the waiting game. Center yourself on your board and let your legs dangle over each side. If you're wobbling around, you are not centered. When you're in the right spot, you will be able to sit comfortably without much movement. And don't be taken off guard: Make sure you are facing the horizon. You want to be aware of what is coming toward you.

Getting into Position

When you see a wave coming, you will need to get into position. Remember, when not riding a wave, you should be facing the horizon. Scoot back on your board so the nose of pops out of the water. Kick your legs in an eggbeater motion as you use a hand to push yourself around (one hand should be holding onto the rail). Once you've turned yourself around, lie down on your board, make sure you are stable and level, and get ready to paddle like the wind.

Taking Off

When an approaching wave is close to breaking, paddle, paddle, paddle—you want your momentum to equal that of the wave by the time the wave reaches you. (Sometimes it's tough to judge if the wave is actually about to break, and if indeed, it's a good wave. Have faith. Eventually your timing and wave selection will get better.) Again, make sure you are centered on your board. If you're too far forward, you will pearl (nose-dive), and if you're too far back, you will stall and probably miss the wave completely. When the wave takes you and you *think* you've got it, give it a few more hard paddles. Once you're absolutely sure you've caught the wave, spring (*pop!*) to your feet and find your balance. Remember: feet slightly wider than your shoulders, knees just bent, hips low, chest up, one foot in front of the other, back foot perpendicular to your board, front foot turned out slightly.

WATCH AND LEARN

When you surf, observe the other surfers in the water. Notice the waves they go for as well as the ones they let roll by. Watch how and when they catch a wave, and take note of their position on the board. When they start carving turns, check out where they place their feet and how they use the rest of their body. Pick up a few surf videos (see the Additional Resources section, page 133, for some suggestions) as well and watch and learn from the comfort of your living room sofa. (Caution: Surf videos are highly addictive.)

Catching the wave:

PAULINE MENCZER: "Make sure YOUR BOARD IS TOTALLY FLAT. If you feel like you're going to miss the wave, as a last-ditch effort, push your chin down on your board."

KIM HAMROCK: "Watch the wave! Look over both shoulders as you are paddling for the wave and PAY ATTENTION to the base or trough of the wave as well as the top pitching part. Get into the wave as it is forming, match the wave speed, and as a general rule, take three extra paddles to make sure you have enough speed to get down the face of the wave."

When you're just starting to surf, try to avoid taking off when the wave has jacked up and is breaking (aka *a late drop*). This will inevitably lead to a nasty wipeout. Look for waves that are steep enough to ride but have yet to crest. The late drops will come later when you're trying to, say, pull into a barrel at Pipeline!

Navigating *Your Board*

In an ideal world, you want to stay just ahead of where the wave is breaking, in the *pocket*. The pocket is where the wave is the steepest and most powerful. Staying in the pocket requires that you ride diagonally with the wave (as opposed to just shooting straight for the beach) as it rolls toward shore. To do so, you need to first rotate your body in the direction you want to ride, then transfer your weight to your back foot and push the tail left if you want to turn right and right if you want to turn left. The degree to which you need to turn your board will depend on how fast the wave is breaking. This is something you will have to judge for yourself. To maintain this position, put pressure on the inside rail (the rail that is facing the wave). If you are surfing with your chest toward the wave, put weight into your front toe, and if you're surfing with your back toward the wave, the weight should be in your front heel. Once you feel comfortable with this basic turn, check out the more advanced turns in "To Cruise: Longboarding Basics," page 86.

Shop•talk:

If the front of your body is oriented toward the wave as you ride it, you are surfing what is called *frontside*. If your back is to the wave, you are surfing *backside*. For most people, going frontside is easier, though many people enjoy the challenge of surfing backside.

Exit *Strategy*

When your ride is over, your first inclination will probably be to jump off your board in celebration—*hurrah, I did it!* Try to resist this urge; though not always possible, a controlled finish is always the best way to go. There are several ways to make a graceful exit. Try turning out over the top of the wave. This will remove you from the wave and drop you behind it. If you're not entirely comfortable with your turning abilities, you can also lean back and put your weight onto the tail of your board—this will slow down your momentum and allow the wave to roll past you.

SPONTANEOUS POST-SURF NASAL DRIP

With some of your more aggressive surf sessions will come the inevitable, spontaneous post-surf nasal drip. You'll be talking to a friend at the copy machine or in a meeting, and bang, water starts running uncontrollably from your nose (and not just a little bit). Don't worry; this is absolutely normal. When you surf, you wipeout, and when you wipeout, water gets lodged in your sinuses. There's no way to avoid this. Some advice: Carry a tissue.

Carla Rowland on sweet revenge:

66 Once one of the boys WAXED MY BOARD WITH SOAP! The waves were so good and it really bummed me out. Anyway, I waxed up my board and paddled to the top of the lineup. Immediately a nice set came right to me. I proceeded to rip it all the way to the beach! It felt GOOD knowing that whoever did that to me saw that I wasn't swayed and overcame the persecution! 99

JULIE COX: "I have embarrassing moments all of the time! Like NOSE-DIVING, SLIPPING ON ROCKS before or after a session with my board, GETTING MY LEASH CAUGHT IN MY HAIR after a wipeout . . . But everyone goes through them, and scoring one good wave erases them all."

MARY OSBORNE: "RUNNING OVER SOMEONE WHEN I WAS LEARNING. Or dinging someone else's board while borrowing it . . . My neighbor Dave Kanarek, also known as 'Big Wave Dave,' was kind enough to lend me one of his surfboards. Every day before surfing I would run into his yard and borrow the same board and every time I returned it there was always a ding. Luckily, Dave is the mellowest guy on Earth so he never got upset and always encouraged me to get back out in the water. (Thanks, Dave!)"

How Long Did You Consider Yourself a Rookie?

BELEN KIMBLE-CONNELLY: "Until I was able to read a wave properly and have CONTROL over my board. So about a good year and a half."

JULIE COX: "Well, I tried to surf when I was eight and every summer until I was sixteen. At sixteen I really got the hang of it, so I considered myself a beginner for EIGHT YEARS."

KIM HAMROCK: "I am still a beginner!!! Figure about a YEAR OR TWO depending on natural ability and amount of time spent in the water."

HEATHER CLARK: "I stood up after my first wave and then after ONE YEAR I was doing provincial contests."

SERENA BROOKE: "Probably A YEAR, nine months to a year. About around the same time it takes to have a baby!"

Chapter 4: To Rip or to Cruise?

Longboarding and shortboarding are two very different schools of surfing. After you're comfortable catching and riding waves on a longboard, you may want to learn how to *really* ride a longboard: enter the cross step, the nose ride, the bottom turn. Or you may want to switch gears altogether and give the fast turns and radical maneuvers of shortboarding a whirl. Either way, you're surfing. Give them both a try and see which one best suits your style and personality.

✦ TO CRUISE:
LONGBOARDING BASICS

Longboarding has its own culture and approach: It's all about style. The best longboarders don't shred; they cruise. The idea isn't to tear the wave apart, but rather to dance with it, gracefully, fluidly. Beyond basic turning and trimming, longboarders work their way up and down the board—cross-stepping, noseriding—with polish and finesse. Though longboarding is still considered to some adrenalin-pumped shortboarders a humdrum, old-school style, board-design innovations coupled with the skill and commitment of today's longboarders has brought the sport a long way. No longer do you point and shoot. With the new, more maneuverable, high-performance longboards, you can really work the wave. While it is true that the size of the board does slow you down a bit and can keep you (well, everyone except Kim Hamrock) out of really powerful surf, it also allows you to enjoy conditions that are less than perfect, catch smaller waves, and have longer rides.

Here are a few basic longboarding techniques to add to your next performance. (Please note: These are general guidelines. All waves are different, so you'll have to adapt your movements to each particular wave. Also note that references to the *inside rail* indicate the rail that is closest to the wall of the wave, while the references to the *outside rail* denote the rail that faces the beach.)

Angled *Takeoff*

This is the simple act of positioning your board in the same direction that the wave is breaking (rather than pointing it directly at the shore). An angled takeoff allows you to get started a little later and on bigger waves without the fear of an impending nosedive. Angling is actually really easy and can greatly improve the quality of your surfing.

angled takeoff

As you paddle for a wave, position your board in the direction the wave is breaking: If the wave's breaking left, angle slightly to the left; if the wave's breaking right, angle slightly to the right. Then paddle, paddle, pop up, and you're off and running with the wave!

Trimming

To stay with the wave, or as they say, cruise down the line, you will need to keep your board in *trim*. This involves slight adjustments (keyword: *slight*)—forward, backward, side to side—of your body weight on the board. Remember, the goal is to maintain your position in the pocket of the wave. If you need to veer slightly right, lean slightly right; slightly left, lean slightly left; slow down, move to the back of the board; speed up, move to the front of the board. Your ride will consist of a series of constant adjustments; try to be fluid and let one movement flow into the next.

Bottom Turn

A *bottom turn* is necessary when you don't angle into the wave but rather drop straight down the face. In order to stay with the wave, you will need to quickly turn to get back up into the pocket. When you are almost to the bottom of the wave, push down on your rear foot, applying pressure on the inside rail while fluidly leaning into the wall of the wave. Keep your knees bent, your head up, and look in the direction you want to turn—your body will follow your eyes. As you come out of the turn, move up on your board and center your weight to reestablish trim.

Top Turn

A *top turn* redirects you from the top of the wave toward the bottom, most likely after a big bottom turn. As you reach the top of the wave, transfer your weight to the back outside rail and shift your head and shoulders in the direction of the turn, bringing the board around with you. As you finish the turn, center your weight over the board.

Cut*back*

You use a *cutback* when you've outrun the breaking part of the wave and need to "cut back" to the pocket. If the wave is breaking to the right, you will cut back to the left; likewise, if it's breaking to the left, you cut back to the right. A cutback is performed from the shoulder of the wave and should be done *before* you run out of speed. Stand at the back of the board with most of your weight in your back foot. Keep your knees bent and loose, hips low, chest up. Lean in the direction you want to turn the board, putting weight on the outside rail. Shift your head and upper body in the same direction, and push your feet forward into the arc of the turn. Once you've completed the turn, level out your board. You'll probably follow a cutback with a mid-face turn to put you back in the direction the wave is breaking.

Kim Hamrock on the top turn:

66 Wait until you get to the top of the wave right where the LIP IS PITCHING. Hit the wave with the flat, bottom part of your board. The farther back you are on the tail of your surfboard, the faster your board will pivot. PIVOT FROM YOUR WAIST, USING YOUR SHOULDERS TO DIRECT WHERE YOU ARE GOING. Just as your board meets the wave, hit the lip and drive your board back down the face of the wave in this twisting motion . . . It is fine to let the wave assist you in turning but you will get more power and speed by driving the board back down the wave. 99

Cross *Step*

A beginning surfer will tend to shuffle up and down the board when adjusting her weight to maintain trim. While this board cha-cha is somewhat effective and fine when you're a beginner, it's, well, unsightly. Once you have your sea legs and feel confident and competent catching and riding waves, it's time to start working on your style. Enter the cross step. *Cross-stepping* is exactly that, crossing one foot over the other as you work your way up the board (for speed) and then back down (to slow down or to reposition for a turn), and is used to help keep your board in trim. It may sound easy, but it actually takes a delicate foot to pull it off and will take some practice and patience to perfect (and even then you'll

the cross step

still wipe out from time to time). Each cross step will of course vary with each wave and with different boards, so you'll need to be agile. Do a little experimenting: Be aware of each step and how your board responds, and keep a mental log of just when you need to step, how quickly or slowly, how widely, and how much pressure to put into each step.

Belen Kimble-Connelly on cross-stepping:

66 **The biggest mistake made with the cross step is that you walk the board when in fact, you should actually be** PULLING THE BOARD WITH YOUR FEET UNDER YOU AND BRINGING THE NOSE TO YOU. 99

DRY RUN

Before attempting the cross step in the water, you may want to first practice it on the beach; just lay your board down in the sand and give it a whirl. And if you can't get to the beach, test your balance and use a curb.

Nose*ride*

Once you've mastered the art of cross-stepping, it's time to take it up a notch to the preeminent noseride: You hovering magically over the water as you stand at the front end of your board. This is the thrill of a lifetime, but you're going to have to earn it. Again, it's a delicate balancing act between you, your board, and the wave, and can only be accomplished under certain circumstances: You are in trim, the wave is nicely lined up, the planets are aligned. First, secure the inside rail and tail in the breaking part of the wave. This will create a balanced and steady stage to strut your stuff. Now, gracefully cross-step your way to the front of the board. Relax, find your balance, and enjoy the ride from the front seat. Step back if at any point you feel the board becoming unstable; otherwise, the tail will flip up and out of the water and will send you forward with it.

If you're feeling really confident, you may want to hang five. This is when you place one foot at the end of your board and hang your five little toes over the end. It will improve your balance if you drop your hips, relax your knees, and put the opposite leg a few feet behind the front foot. Child's play, you say? Fine. It's time to hang ten—a very difficult maneuver but huge on the style scoreboard. Place both feet at the very nose of your board so all ten toes peek off the end; stay relaxed, loose, and ready to step back the second your board wavers. Smile and wave to the crowd. Don't wipe out.

Carla Rowland on noseriding:

66 TOES MUST BE OVER THE NOSE to be considered a true noseride! Stretching your foot 6 inches from the nose and throwing your hands in the air does not count! 99

Margeaux Hamrock on her first noseride:

66 When I was ten years old we went to Tamarindo, Costa Rica. I had just started to ride open-face waves and I was getting used to the transition. I had been cross-stepping in the whitewater for quite sometime and had the hang of it, so I thought I should try cross-stepping on the open-face wave. On my first try I went all the way to the nose and I stood there in complete shock: I WAS NOSERIDING! I LOOKED DOWN AT MY FEET AND I FELT LIKE I WAS FLYING. The nose of my board started to go under and I cross-stepped back and then I kicked out. IT WAS THE BEST FEELING I HAD EVER EXPERIENCED. The best part was that my mom got the whole ride on video. Noseriding is still my favorite part of surfing. 99

hanging five

✦ TO RIP:
SHORTBOARDING BASICS

In the late sixties, shortboards came on the scene and drastically changed the world of surfing. With this lighter, shorter board came greater maneuverability, faster turns, and the ability to perform—rather than just survive—on bigger, steeper, hollower waves. Unlike longboarding with its cross step, noserides, and trimming, shortboarding, involves very little actual movement on the board, but rather uses slight shifts in body weight to maneuver the board. For most shortboarders, the idea is to rip (shred, carve) the wave apart. Similar to longboarding, there's a fluidity and grace to shortboarding; it's just in high gear.

Board Transition: *The Honest Truth*

A typical shortboard is usually just north of 6 feet—that's roughly 3 feet shorter than your average longboard. It's narrower, thinner, has more rocker, and a pointed nose, which translates to greater difficulty paddling, popping up, and catching waves. Be prepared; board transition is hard. You will get frustrated, you will miss a lot of waves, you will wipe out (a lot). Okay, bad news over. Good news: You'll get it. Just practice.

THE FUNBOARD

You may want to take some of the sting out of your transition from a longboard to a shortboard with a funboard. It's a hybrid of the two boards—longer than a shortboard (around 7 feet) but slightly narrower and thinner than a longboard—so you get a certain amount of longboard stability with more shortboard maneuverability. Or you may be more of a masochist and choose to go directly from a longboard to a shortboard. It's entirely up to you.

The **Pop-Up** Revisited

When transitioning to a shortboard, you may have to modify how you pop up from the prone to standing position. With a longboard, your feet rest nicely on the end of the board as you're paddling, so you can use them to push off as you swing your legs underneath you. But you'll notice on a shortboard, the feet dangle off the end of the board, which renders them utterly useless, so instead, the knees must act as the fulcrum. *Attention:* This does not mean crawl to your knees and then get up—that would be impossible on a fast-moving shortboard anyway! This motion is the exact same—quick, fluid, smooth, unified—as the one you have practiced on your longboard, but the feel is a little different and something you may have to get used to.

The following exercise simulates the shortboard pop-up and is great practice for the real thing. Lay on your bed with your feet and ankles dangling off the end. Now, pop up. Remember: It's one, seamless movement. Push yourself away from the bed as you arch your back and simultaneously pull your feet and legs underneath you. Notice how you are forced to launch yourself from your knees instead of your feet. This may feel strange at first, but if you practice, practice, practice, you'll eventually get the hang of it, and the transition from a longer board to a shorter board will be that much smoother.

Paddling

Paddling on a shortboard will feel a little awkward at first and will take a bit more oomph than you're probably used to, especially when you're trying to catch a wave. But never fear, with time you will get stronger and the paddling will become smoother and less difficult. Again, head and chest up, legs together and hanging still in the water (not flailing around wasting energy and decreasing efficiency), body centered, elbows bent, hands slightly cupped. Try not to rock back and forth, but rather, plane across the water, keeping the nose of the board about 2 inches above the water.

Duck-*Dive*

Now you've got to get out to the lineup. Sure, the turtle still works, but if you want to be taken seriously as a shortboarder, you should learn how to *duck-dive*. When you duck-dive, you, along with your board, are essentially diving under the wave and popping out its backside. The entire action should resemble one enormous scooping motion. If you've spent any time playing in the surf, you've probably done a similar motion with your body. The key: Get yourself and your board down as deep as humanly possible when the wave passes over you, and then direct the buoyancy of your board to pull you up and out the wave's backside.

Here's the breakdown. As the wave approaches, paddle hard—the more speed the better. When it's a few feet in front of you, grab the rails of your board at your chest, and push down (as if doing a push-up) using your body weight to submerge the board. After driving the front of the board down with your hands, push down on the tail with your knee or foot. As the wave passes over you, angle the board up slightly (about 45 degrees), flattening yourself against the board—the more streamlined the better (remember, you are directing the buoyancy of your board to pull you and the board up and out the wave's backside). Bang, you're out. Start paddling.

On the duck-dive:

PAULINE MENCZER: *"MAKE SURE YOU START EARLY!* Push with your arms first and just as you feel that the board won't go down any further, push the back of the board with your foot or knee.*"*

HEATHER CLARK: *"*You cannot perfect a duck-dive, depending on the wave and how big and powerful it is, you can always get thrown around or taken back a few feet ... *I ALWAYS OPEN MY EYES AS I AM COMING UP* so I can watch the wave go over me and see where there is a pocket or gap so I can angle my board into that clear water and up I pop.*"*

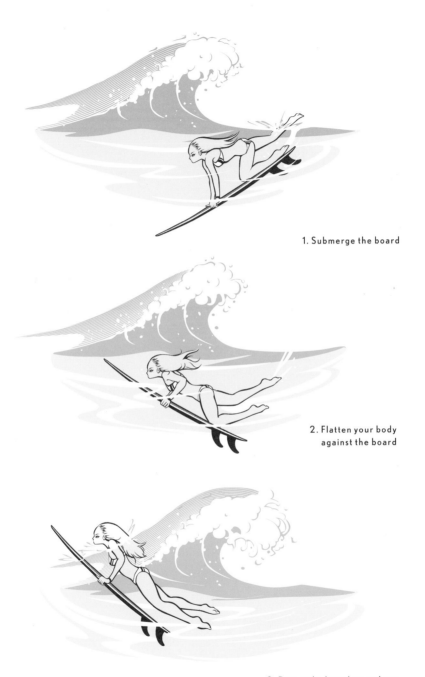

1. Submerge the board

2. Flatten your body
against the board

3. Direct the board up and out

A seasoned surfer can and will duck-dive waves up to 12 feet. For any chance of surfing bigger, more critical waves, you will need to learn how to duck-dive. Without this skill, it will be nearly impossible, if not impossible, to successfully make it out to the lineup.

Frieda Zamba on maintaining a sense of humor:

66 When I was an up-and-coming surfer on the tour I was in Japan for a contest and Kim Mearig was the hot surf girl to beat. Everybody was all about Kim, taking pictures, asking for autographs, and nobody paid attention to me. I REMEMBER THINKING, ONE DAY I'LL GET MY SHOT AND ONE DAY THEY'LL KNOW MY NAME. I was out there freesurfing and Kim and a bunch of other pro girls were out as well, and all of these Japanese girls were standing on the beach waiting for Kim. She went in and signed some autographs and then left the beach. I came in shortly after and saw a bunch of Japanese girls running towards me. THEY WERE SCREAMING 'KIM, KIM, KIM!' I'M LIKE, 'NO, I'M NOT KIM' (Kim and I both had yellow boards and blonde hair), but they just kept going 'Kim, Kim, please sign!' and I'm thinking, well, if they're not smart enough to know what Kim looks like then I'll just give them what they want, and I signed Kim Mearig's name on T-shirts, posters, hats, etc., for the rest of the contest . . . When they announced my name for my heat I'm sure there were some confused Japanese girls . . . I wonder what Kim thought when she saw a kid go by with her signature on their sweatshirt and it wasn't her handwriting. 99

Taking Off

The *takeoff* on a shortboard is a whole new experience. Because the board is less buoyant, it's nearly impossible to generate enough speed to catch a wave by simply paddling into it; you'll need to use the energy from the wave (along with a lot of strong, aggressive paddling) in order to make it. This means taking off when circumstances are a little

Pauline Menczer on perfecting your stance:

66 First get your feet right: The back foot over the middle fins and the front foot a little bit back from the middle of the board. YOUR WEIGHT SHOULD BE OVER THE CENTER OF THE BOARD AND YOUR KNEES SHOULD BE BENT. 99

bit dicier—as the wave is cresting—so your timing needs to be a lot more precise than when you're riding a longboard. As the wave approaches and starts to crest, spin around, get centered on your board, and paddle with purpose; when you feel the wave start to take you, this is your cue to lean forward and really give it some muscle—dig, dig, dig (you may even want do a few kicks with your feet). It will be scary and you will be freaked out, but you can do it. Just take a deep breath and charge. When you're certain you've caught the wave, pop up. Once you're up, have expertly managed the drop, you may need to do a bottom turn (see page 102) to get yourself properly positioned in the pocket.

Rochelle Ballard on fear:

66 I grew up in Kauai and had to grow up surfing on reef breaks, so the learning curve was steep and quick. I was always afraid. It was the guys I grew up with who pushed me and kind of sent me over the edge, enticing me, teasing me to go, and it really paid off. THE BEST WAY TO OVERCOME FEAR IS EXPERIENCE. To me fear is the unknown, and once you start to learn about the things that you fear, they are no longer as scary. Even now my heart still races, but I have an understanding of the wave, I know what to do, where to go, so that makes it less intimidating.

Having the experience and making yourself feel comfortable in the place you don't know, learning what you need to know, starting to understand it, will help you deal with your fear. I think this applies to anything in life. 99

bottom turn

Bottom Turn

You may need to make a *bottom turn* after the drop to get back into the pocket, to set up for another turn, or yes, in time, to get barreled. After you drop down the face of the wave, first put pressure on your back foot and then rotate your weight to the inside rail, angling your body toward the wall of the wave. Even out your weight on the inside rail, keeping your knees bent and your hips low. When you've completed the turn, center your weight on the board. Take note: You are not moving your feet around on the board, just transferring your weight forward and backward, side to side—this is the case for all of the shortboard turns.

Top Turn

A *top turn* redirects you into the wave, usually after a big bottom turn. Before the introduction of the aerial (launching yourself off the lip of the wave—hold your horses, this will come *much* later), a well-timed top turn was the acme of shortboard ripping, and executing a good one will still earn you solid style points. Use your speed to race to the top of the wave. Just as you hit the lip, rotate your weight to the back outside rail of your board and quickly shift your head and shoulders in the direction of the turn, bringing the board around with you. As you finish the turn, center your weight over the board.

Cutback

When you attempt a *cutback,* you will be turning from the shoulder of the wave back toward the breaking part of the wave. This turn will help you reposition yourself for speed in the pocket. From the wave's shoulder, turn away from the wall of the wave, rotating your head and shoulders toward the breaking part of the wave and leaning into your back outside rail. Carry your speed. Let your front arm guide you and look in the direction you want to go. As you come about, maintain a balanced stance and roll your weight back over the center of the board. A mid-face turn will put you back into trim.

top turn

cutback

66 The main thing to do is REPLACE THE FEAR
OR INTIMIDATION THING WITH
FUN AND EXCITEMENT.
Say you can shortboard, but you've had something
happen that was scary or discouraging. Take a step back.
Go out on a longboard. TAKE THE ANXIETY
AWAY AND JUST REALLY HAVE FUN IN
THE OCEAN AGAIN. Then ease yourself back
into shortboarding. **99**

Speed *Cuts*

In shortboarding, speed is everything. The quality of your surfing will depend greatly on generating enough speed to make your turns and keep up with the wave. Speed cuts are the art of effectively using your body weight and gravity coupled with the steep section of the wave to generate enough momentum to run with the wave. Simplistically, they are a series of ever-so-slight bottom and top turns—also known as "pump" turns or "pumping"—that run one into the next (if you were to draw a series of speed cuts, your sketch would look like a slithering snake). You will need to learn how to do this or your shortboarding will really suffer—it's all about speed, kid—so pay attention. The idea is to float to the top of the wave and bomb back down, float to the top, bomb back down, fluidly, effortlessly, generating more and more speed with each turn (or cut). Try to keep your weight slightly forward. Lighten pressure on the board as you ascend the wave, and then throw your weight into it as you descend.

Chapter 5:
Etiquette and Safety

✦ CODE OF CONDUCT

Once you hit the water, there are some strict road rules that every surfer (even the greenest of rookies) *must* know to ensure that everyone has fun and stays safe. Make sure you are familiar with the following codes of conduct *before* your maiden voyage; it is assumed that if you're out in the lineup, you know and live by these rules. People who don't follow the code not only endanger themselves, but are also a hazard for the other people in the water. All of this elaborate etiquette may seem a bit overwhelming at first, but in time, these rules will become second nature, and you'll see just how much they really do help make a better, safer, more fun environment for everyone.

Kim Hamrock on first-timers to the lineup:

❝ BE READY! Know the rules of surf etiquette and be sure you already have good **CONTROL OF YOUR BOARD.** WAIT YOUR TURN, THERE IS A PECKING ORDER OUT THERE. Start by catching leftover waves (the ones others miss) and the smaller inside waves, slowly working your way CLOSER TO THE PEAK. **❞**

Beginner *Bastion*

Get yourself off on the right foot by picking an appropriate spot to surf. If you're just starting the sport, find a known beginner location. If you're not sure, ask the folks in the local surf shop; they'll know just where to steer you. At a beginner spot you'll find waves that are suitable for your level of experience and you won't have to battle other, more experienced and aggressive surfers for waves. You'll also be surrounded by fellow kooks (that's surf-speak for beginners), who tend to be more understanding when you blow a wave or inadvertently drop in on them. More advanced spots are obviously home to more advanced surfers who expect the other surfers out there to at least have a grasp of what they're doing, and who are not the most forgiving when you prove otherwise. Stay clear of these spots until your skills improve and you can really enjoy them.

Paddling *Out*

Okay, you've settled on an appropriate spot, you're standing at the water's edge, your leash is tightly secured around the correct ankle, you've assessed the surf and have found the best place to paddle out (remember, the path of least resistance), and your muscles are twitching with adrenaline—it's time to get wet. Keep the following in mind as you paddle your way out to the lineup.

First and foremost, stay out of the way. If people are catching waves in as you are paddling out, paddle around the break to avoid ruining someone's ride or worse, a head-on collision. If this is impossible, then paddle toward the whitewater of the breaking wave. Always paddle away from oncoming surfer; never, ever paddle directly into his or her path. If you panic and aren't sure what to do, stop paddling, stay put, and let the oncoming surfer ride by.

LOCALS RULE

Locals are people who live near and regularly surf one spot. They therefore consider it quite definitively *their* spot and are highly aware and suspect of newcomers to the lineup. Some locals can be nasty and territorial, true (this is called *localism*), but more often than not, with some time, most locals are willing to share their wave with a polite and competent surfer. The bottom line: Show respect and eventually you will be respected.

The Lineup

Once you've made it out to the lineup, you'll want to abide by the lineup manifesto: Don't crowd, don't park yourself on the outside, and don't loiter too far on the inside. Situate yourself so that you're just about even with everyone else. (And give yourself and those around you some room to breathe.) Sit too far outside and you'll indicate to the others in the lineup that you're a selfish wave hog trying to catch the waves before anyone else has the chance (major no-no). Sit too far on the inside and you'll probably be in the way when someone else catches a wave. Find a happy medium somewhere among the bobbing heads and go from there.

Carla Rowland on lineup etiquette:

66 **Treat it like a freeway. Look both ways before merging.** DON'T CUT PEOPLE OFF. NEVER JUST STOP IN THE MIDDLE OF THE LINEUP. IF YOU CAN, TRY TO NOTE WHO THE LOCAL OR BETTER SURFERS ARE; RESPECT THEM and LEARN FROM THEM. 99

Taking Off

When you've spotted a wave you want to go for, make sure you first check to see if anyone else has priority over you. The general rule: The person closest to the peak (the breaking part of the wave) has the right to the wave. If that's *not* you, don't go. When you've started to paddle for the wave but before you pop up, look left and right. If someone is up and riding behind you, it's their wave—no questions asked—so pull out. If someone's in front of you (this is known as *dropping in*), give a loud whistle or a firm "yo!" to let them know it's your wave and they should pull out. Dropping in (aka snaking, burning, or cutting off) is a major surfing faux pas. Don't do it. If you inadvertently do drop in on someone (it happens from time to time—excitement can get the best

surfing's cardinal sin: dropping in

of us), a simple apology will go a long way. However, keep in mind that repeat offenders are usually not welcomed back to the lineup, so don't make it a habit.

EXCUSING YOURSELF, GRACEFULLY

If you're paddling for a wave but quickly realize it's not yours for the taking, just sit back on your board. This can be done gracefully and without much fuss, and it will quickly pull you out of the wave, rightfully clearing the path for the deserving surfer behind you. If you've already caught the wave and are standing, leaning your weight on the back of the board will achieve the same effect.

GET A GRIP

A loose board is a dangerous board for you and for those around you; make sure whenever possible you hold onto your board. First try grabbing the rails. If it's too late for that, grab the leash immediately after you fall and quickly pull the board toward you.

✦ STAYING SAFE

Surfing is an amazing, gratifying, and thrilling experience; in short, it rules. But the ocean is a force of nature, literally, and can be unpredictable, powerful, and turbulent (not to mention full of lots of beautiful but frisky sea creatures), so you need to take some precautions when you surf and know what to do if and when your safety is jeopardized.

Assess the Conditions

First off, make sure you choose the appropriate break (beach, point, reef) for your skill level; a 5-foot pounding beachbreak is a far cry from a 5-foot mushy pointbreak. Know what you're getting yourself into *before* you paddle out. If you're new to the spot, take a minute to ask locals or lifeguards if there are any hazards you should be aware of and then give the area a quick once-over for yourself.

Be very aware of wave size and changing conditions. The ocean is a miraculous thing—one minute the waves are small and harmless, a few hours later huge booming monsters are roaring in. You do not want to get caught in over your head—it can be dangerous and quite terrifying—so do your research. Start by lobbing a call in to the surf or buoy report. They can give you at least a general idea of the size and conditions, and how the surf will be trending for the day. And once you're at the beach, spend ten or fifteen minutes—enough time to witness a few sets roll in—just watching. How big are the waves? How are they breaking? How shallow is the water? Where is the best place to paddle out? Then use your best judgment.

Stay Alert

The ocean is constantly shifting. After you've paddled out, it's very important that you remain aware of and responsive to the changing conditions. There may be a current that's pulling you down the beach (or worse yet, out to sea), or perhaps the tide has reached its low point, making it dangerously shallow to surf. Recognize these potential dangers and act accordingly.

Surfing Solo

For the beginning surfer, surfing alone, entirely alone, is not a good idea. Accidents do happen, and you'll definitely want someone, *anyone*, around to help you out if necessary. This does not mean, however, that you can't surf on your own, i.e., without your loud or highly caffeinated or always-running-late friends. A solo mission can be a meditative, therapeutic getaway, and for some a ritual. It is safe if other surfers, even just one, are also in the water with you. Though they may sometimes seem aloof and dismissive, surfers in the lineup *do* look out for each other.

Rip *Currents*

Rip currents are formed when excess water gets caught near shore and then forces its way back out to sea in an effort to balance the water level. They're easy to spot: a mass of choppy water (*sans* waves) flowing in one direction—out to sea. While this action can help pull you out to the lineup, be forewarned that some rip currents are *extremely* powerful and should be avoided. (A good friend and veteran surfer was pointedly reminded of this, finding himself having to hitch a ride with the Ocean Beach Coast Guard after getting sucked out to sea by a rip.) If you get caught in a strong rip current, don't panic and start furiously paddling for the beach: That's futility at its purest. To break free, paddle parallel to the beach, and once out of the current, turn for shore.

✦ JAWS AND FRIENDS

Yes, it's true: You are not the only one out there. Lots and lots of little and not-so-little (huge, actually) creatures are swimming, floating, and crawling beneath you as you surf. Give yourself a moment to freak out—*freaking out!*—now pull yourself together. For the most part they won't even notice you. Here's how to deal if you should have a chance encounter.

Sharks

Not much you can do here. Accept it. They are lurking out there—big, scary, hungry—but, really, in the whole grand scheme of things, they are not a huge threat. A few suggestions, however: Do heed local warnings. Obviously, if a shark was spotted cruising your local break and swimming has been temporarily banned, don't sneak out for an illicit sunset session. Do get out of the water if you've been wounded and are bleeding—sharks can smell blood from very far away—and do avoid areas where fisherman have been chumming. Do not surf near seal colonies and be aware that sharks are partial to river mouths. If you're in the water and a shark has been spotted (*relax*, this most likely will not happen, but just in case . . .), do not thrash about and draw attention to yourself. Instead paddle calmly, quietly, and quickly for the shore.

rip current

66 I was in Durban, well a fifteen-minute car drive from Durban, and was surfing with lots of surfers. We watched this fin that was kind of floppy go by. The *"SHARK"* turned around and the fin went really straight and stiff. It came towards a group of us and then just disappeared under the water. No one sat around— *WE ALL PADDLED LIKE CRAZY TO THE BEACH!* 99

Stingrays

These guys are flat, streamlined bottom feeders with a venomous barb (or barbs) on the end of their whiplike tails. They can be found in shallow water close to shore and are a potential hazard if you're wading out. Camouflaged in the sand, they can be tough to spot and easily stepped on if you're not careful. To reduce the risk of a sting, make sure you shuffle your feet as you wade out. This will alert the stingrays in the area that you are approaching, and they'll usually swim off to calmer waters (their sting is defensive, not offensive). If you do get hit, you'll experience a lot of pain and some swelling. Make sure you soak your foot in really, really hot water (as hot as you can stand) for about thirty minutes and remove any stinger left in the skin.

Sea Urchins

You will generally find sea urchins—a marble- to fist-sized ball with long spikes—nestled on reefs or rocks. You may have a run-in if you're wading out or if you inadvertently put your feet down on the bottom. It's pretty much like getting a really big splinter or jabbing yourself with a pencil lead. There will be some pain and swelling, and sometimes the tip of the spike will break off in your foot. Soak your foot in really hot water for fifteen minutes, and if possible, remove the spike with tweezers. If the spike(s) are too small for removal, don't fret; they will dissolve in a few weeks. Apply antibiotic ointment.

Jellyfish *and* Portuguese Man-o'-Wars

These guys can actually be rather beautiful—translucent, graceful, almost ethereal—but wow, do they hurt. While their beauty lies in part in their gelatinous translucence, it also makes them very difficult to see, and you may be stung unawares. Different jellyfish give out different stings. Depending on the severity, you may experience stinging, itching, redness, rash, and in some cases, fever, nausea, and vomiting. If the tentacle breaks off and is stuck to you, use a dull butter knife, a credit card, or something of that nature, to remove the tentacle from your skin—do your best not to touch it with your fingers. Wipe down the area with alcohol and then coat it with meat tenderizer—this will destroy the toxins left by the jellyfish. Leave that on for twenty minutes. Wipe down the area again with alcohol and apply hydrocortisone cream. On occasion, some people may experience a serious allergic reaction called anaphylactic shock—symptoms are throat or tongue swelling, difficulty breathing, elevated pulse, sweating, dizziness. If this happens, call 911 immediately!

Water *Pollution*

One of the greatest dangers to surfers these days is not the man-o'-war or the sea urchin or even the shark. It's actually a much bigger, manmade threat: water pollution. It's in the water, every day, surrounding you, and it's making a lot of surfers sick. It comes in the form of sewage, pesticides, herbicides, and other toxic chemicals that run off into beach storm drains after it rains or are shamelessly dumped into the ocean or nearby creeks or rivers that empty into the ocean. No scare tactics are being used here, just the simple truth. If you plan to be in the water a lot, it's a good idea to do some investigating. Check with lifeguards, locals, or the Surfrider Foundation (www.surfrider.org) to find out just how safe the water is in your area and then use your best judgment. Some areas of Los Angeles County, California, for example, are notorious for their polluted waters, and many surfers avoid the water after an especially heavy rain.

✦ OTHER DANGERS

Reef Cuts

While reefbreaks can create some of the greatest waves in the world, an unfortunate brush with the coral can cause abrasions and occasionally deep cuts in the skin. When coupled with the bacteria in the water and the coral itself, they can lead to a serious infection. If you find yourself with a cut, immediately wash it with fresh water and soap. Douse it a few times with a bit of drugstore variety hydrogen peroxide and gently pat dry. Now take a deep breath, bite your lip, and apply a few drops of iodine (colorless iodine is available if you don't like the pink stuff). It will sting, and quite badly. Scream if it helps. Allow to dry. Apply a layer of antibiotic ointment. Watch for infection—it happens easily—and depending on the severity of the cut, you might want to stay out of the water a few days (if you can stand it).

Surfboard Cuts

A surfboard fin can cut like a knife. Some surfers will sand down the edges of their fins slightly so they aren't quite as sharp. (After a center fin decisively sliced the rump of my wetsuit wide open, I did.) If you do get cut, follow the same drill as with reef cuts: wash, dry, douse with hydrogen peroxide, apply iodine, scream, apply antibiotic ointment. Please note: There are rubber-edged fins available, which are safer. If you're a beginner, they are a must-have.

Spinal Injury

A spinal injury will most likely occur in shallow water. Though they happen infrequently, it's best that you know how to quickly and effectively deal with them on the rare chance that the worst does happen. If you suspect a fellow surfer has a spinal injury, first check her vital signs: Is she responsive? Does she have a pulse? Is she breathing? If no, immediately begin CPR. If yes, calm her down and comfort her as you move on to in-line stabilization—minimizing movement of the spine. (Obviously, someone else has or is calling 911.) Treat the head, neck, and back as one complete unit or block, trying your best not to move any part individually. Be gentle in your movements and don't jostle the victim. If possible, use your surfboard as a backboard, and remove her from the surf zone as quickly and smoothly as possible.

LIFESAVER

If you plan to spend a lot of time around the water, at the least, you should get your first aid and CPR certifications. Check with your local American Red Cross chapter or their Web site, www.redcross.org for more information. And while you're at it, a class in aquatic safety and emergencies wouldn't be a bad call either.

Chapter 6: **Travel**

✦ THE CALL OF THE WILD

Be prepared for your budding surfing obsession to eventually draw you across state lines, continents, and oceans; through multiple time zones, airports, and tiny, isolated towns; and down dusty, bumpy roads, just to surf. These trips have the potential to provide the experience and the waves of a lifetime if you do your research and are properly prepared.

By Car

You don't have to fly to some exotic location to find good surf: It could be just a car ride away. Don't forget about neighboring towns, states, and countries when pulling together a surf trip. Sometimes a road trip with a gaggle of girls is more than enough to scratch your surfing itch and satisfy your need for adventure.

pre-trip planning: The amount you have to pre-plan will depend greatly on how far you're driving and whether or not you know much about the destination. Obviously, take this into consideration when organizing your trip and give yourself enough time to adequately pull it all together.

finding surf: If you're not familiar with the destination and are not exactly sure where to find waves, check out www.surfmaps.com or *The Stormrider Guide North America* for potential spots (see Additional Resources, pages 133 and 136, for details). And once you arrive, hit the local surf shop and pick the guys there for info.

packing: Pack light. You *will* end up wearing pretty much the same outfit every day—it always happens—and there's no need for extra baggage. Don't forget to bring something warm for the evenings (sweatshirt, pants, beanie) especially if you're camping, and beyond your flip-flops, a pair of sneakers and socks is a good idea for mosquito protection and impromptu walks. Be practical. Only pack nice clothes if you're planning a night on the town. Chances are you'll be spending most of your evenings bouncing on a hotel bed or huddled around a campfire, so white low-riders are just not necessary, no matter how cute they are.

+ Cell phones to be used only in cases of emergency.
+ Good music must be played at high volume at all times (singing along is encouraged).
+ Absolutely no farting without appropriate ventilation.
+ Snacks and beverages must be readily available.
+ There must be at least one extensive conversation about bikini waxing.
+ Even the mere mention of work is prohibited.
+ No studying!
+ No monopolizing shotgun.
+ Men must be discussed in excruciating detail.
+ Trashy magazines must be read, celebrities scrutinized.
+ Most embarrassing surf moments must be shared.

PREPARING THE SURF MOBILE

insurance: If you're driving from California or Texas to Mexico, you will need special car insurance. You can find insurance providers nestled near the U.S. side of the border if you want to deal with it on your way, or you can always handle it over the Internet beforehand.

racks: You will of course need racks for your car if you don't already have them. You can either make the investment and buy a permanent rack, or go with the soft rack. For more information, see page 55.

tunes: An absolute must for any road trip; CD library must be stocked and DJ delegated.

surf coffer: This should already be a permanent fixture in your car, but just in case you're a little behind, see page 56.

+ We have insurance.
+ We have snacks.
+ We have beverages.
+ We have tunes.
+ We have magazines.
+ The boards *are* strapped down.
+ The wetsuits are packed (if necessary).
+ The car has a full tank; the oil has been changed; the tires are pumped.
+ Bags are in the trunk and not on the curb.
+ Surf coffer is stocked and loaded.
+ Cell phones are off.
+ Everyone has gone to the bathroom and is actually in the car.
+ Green light: Go!

By Plane

Traveling to distant locales—Peru, Tonga, Sri Lanka, Senegal, Indonesia—in search of surf is an amazing way to see the world, meet new people, and, of course, find the perfect right pointbreak (or left pointbreak or barreling reefbreak or whatever it is your little heart desires). With just a bit of research and planning, you're on you way to paradise, and most likely, the ride of your life.

Prepackaged Surf Trips

There are several companies out there that offer prepackaged surf trips. The packages vary, but you can expect most to include accommodations, transportation, a surf guide, alternative activities, maps, tidal charts, recommended restaurants, and travel advice—you're pretty much only responsible for buying your plane ticket and making your flight. If you're not familiar with an area, a prepackaged deal may be the best (and safest) introduction to the surf and the country. Check out the list of companies and their Web sites in the Additional Resources section, page 135, for more information.

Boat Trips

A boat trip could be considered a prepackaged surf trip, but there is one huge difference: You are on a boat, and not just for a few days, but for the entire trip—usually about ten days. The boat trip is really for the surfing diehard (when not eating or sleeping, you are surfing), so if you're looking for a more well-rounded vacation, it is probably not for you. The beauty of the boat trip is two-fold: You surf breaks only accessible by boat—meaning fewer crowds—and many of these breaks are some of the best, most breathtaking in the world. There are usually about eight surfers on the boat, a cook, some crew, and a captain (and maybe his family). You can sign up for a boat solo but risk being stuck—on a boat—with seven people you may or may not like or, you can gather a posse of your girlfriends and book an entire boat for yourselves. Up to you. See the Additional Resources section, page 135, for more information.

Surf Schools

There are hundreds of surf schools scattered throughout the world and more popping up every day (some are exclusively for women, others are co-ed). Depending on your time availability, attending surf school may be something you want to do over a long weekend—some schools offer "the weekend getaway"—or something you want to commit to for a week or more. Surf school can be an excellent excuse for a vacation and is a fantastic way to learn how to surf: professional instruction, beautiful location, supportive environment, and more often than not, perfect, little waves. And some schools offer "the spa atmosphere," which includes yoga, massage, and probably some tofu, if you're into that. See the Additional Resources section, page 135, for suggestions and locations.

boat trip: for the surfing diehard

Information *Gathering*

Do your research! Understanding the people and culture of a different country—before you go—will not only make your trip more interesting, it will also keep you safer. And bear in mind, some of the world's greatest surf spots are also home to some of the world's greatest turmoil, so make sure you're not flying into the middle of a political uprising or a religious revolt just to get a good surf—it's not worth it. (For State Department warnings see: http://travel.state.gov/travel/warnings.html.)

Some travel suggestions from Heather Clark:

 ALWAYS TAKE A SPARE CHANGE OF CLOTHES IN YOUR BACKPACK—

no matter how short the trip! (It's amazing HOW MANY PEOPLE'S LUGGAGE GOES MISSING and they have to sit around without a change of clothing.) And don't forget your ear plugs for the plane. **99**

DIG FOR DETAILS

If you know anyone who has been to your destination, pump them for information: good hotels, tasty restaurants, especially fun breaks, non-surf-related activities, nightlife, the local vibe. Chances are they will be more than happy to share their experiences and suggestions with you—surfers *love* talking about their trips.

Shots and Immunizations

Most foreign countries recommend a number of immunizations, but do not necessarily mandate them by law. It's still a good idea to get them, especially if you plan to wander off the beaten track (and if you're looking for surf, you *will* wander). Check with the Centers for Disease Control and Prevention for current recommendations (www.cdc.gov/travel). If you intend to get immunized, plan ahead; some immunization require more than one injection and some cannot be given at the same time, so allow at least the recommended six weeks before your trip to complete your immunizations. And make sure you keep a record of all of your immunizations in an International Health Certificate available from your physician or government health departments as proof of your pain—some countries may ask to see it.

SWELL SEASON

Every surf destination has a time of year when the conditions are at their best. Make sure to book your trip when there's actually going to be swell. Though you can never know for sure, scheduling your trip at the right time of year will definitely up your chances for getting good waves.

Packing

Again, pack only what you need (most likely, a bathing suit, flip-flops, and your board!). Remember, in addition to your luggage you will also be hauling around an enormous board bag, so you're going to want to streamline your stuff. Do bring a long-sleeve shirt and pants for evening mosquito protection and do not forget a hat, sunscreen, and your rash guard for sun protection—you will need it.

Also make sure to check the water temperature of your destination and pack the appropriate wax, and you may also want to stash an extra leash and leash string in your board bag in case yours snaps (in some areas, surf shops are hard to come by).

PARADISE FOUND

For a detailed discussion of various international surf destinations, check out www.surfmaps.com and *The World Stormrider Guide* (see Additional Resources, page 133, for more information).

Packing *Your* Board

Pack your board well. Baggage handlers can be less than gentle, and you don't want to get a ding before your trip even begins. Follow the steps below and your board should arrive safe and sound.

1. Remove your fins. If your fins are glassed in, place a large piece of foam in between them. Make sure the foam extends a few inches beyond the fins—you want it (not the fins) to completely absorb any pressure that may come during transport.

2. If you have a board sock, put it on your board; if not, wrap your board in a few towels, then place bubble wrap around the nose, tail, and rails of your board.

3. If you're taking more than one board, be sure to place something such as a wetsuit or another towel between the boards.

4. Finally, stuff whatever clothes that don't fit in your bag into your board bag for extra protection, zip her up, and you're ready to roll.

This is a seemingly arbitrary figure that the person at the airline ticket counter invents when you eagerly arrive with an enormous board bag. Be prepared; most airlines will charge you up to a hundred bucks *each way*—gasp!—to check your boards. You can call in advance and inquire about the price, but depending on who you talk to, the specific airport, the plane's cargo space, the alignment of the planets, the direction of the wind, etc., it may be tough to get a straight answer. Be friendly and accommodating and hope for the best. (And it is always a good idea to keep your baggage-charge receipt as well; if they try to jack up the price on the return flight you can wave it in their face and say, "No, I don't think so.")

Veteran traveler Serena Brooke suggests:

❝ When they try and charge you a million dollars for your boards, tell them you don't have a credit card or any extra cash on you to pay the charges they're asking for. It usually starts off at like $1000 and then ends up being more like $50. NEVER JUST PAY WHAT THEY FIRST ASK FOR. YOU CAN TALK YOUR WAY OUT OF IT OR GET THEM TO DROP THE FEE . . .

I actually sit and look for the right person before I go up to the counter, who's in a good mood, who looks cool, try to read each person and wait for the right one. It usually ends up being a guy. They're easy. ❞

✦ ONCE YOU'RE THERE

Staying *Healthy*

If you're going to get sick, it's most likely going to be from something you eat or drink. Be cognizant of what you put in your mouth and trust your instincts—if it looks bad or you're wary for any reason, put the fork down and back away from the plate. Only drink water from a bottle with an intact seal, be careful of fruit juices that may have been mixed with water, and don't forget about ice—make sure it's also made from bottled water. Boiling water is an easy way to purify it if you don't have a bottled water source nearby. Milk and other dairy products should be pasteurized. The familiar bottles you find at the grocery should be fine. As for the food, eat only meats that are well cooked, avoid shellfish, and wash and peel your fruits and veggies.

The *Dreaded* Diarrhea

When it does happen (and it might), you may be tempted to take something to help stop it—don't, this will only prolong the problem. Diarrhea is essentially your body flushing itself out, so your best bet is to ride it out. You may be surprised by the severity of your diarrhea (which can be coupled with cramps, nausea, vomiting, chills, and high fever), but it usually only lasts one to three days, so hang in there, you'll live, just make sure you do your best to rehydrate.

REHYDRATION COCKTAIL

If you can't come by any Gastrolyte or other pre-made rehydration mixes, you can easily make your own. Combine and drink the following to help rebalance your electrolytes and get your system back in order.

- ✦ 1 quart water
- ✦ ½ teaspoon baking soda
- ✦ ½ teaspoon table salt
- ✦ 3 tablespoons sugar

GLORIOUS GARLIC:

Besides tasting great in pasta or on bread, garlic has well-known medicinal value: Among other things, it wards off mosquitoes, disinfects wounds, and helps prevent intestinal parasites—so eat as much as you can. If you can't bear to eat garlic raw, there are garlic pills available in grocery and health food stores. Start taking them a good week before your trip so your body is already pumped with garlic when you arrive, and continue your garlic regimen for remainder of your stay.

AT-A-GLANCE PRECAUTIONS

- ✦ Don't eat or drink raw dairy products; look for items that are clearly marked "pasteurized."
- ✦ Make sure your meats are well cooked.
- ✦ Avoid shellfish.
- ✦ Peel and wash your fruit and veggies.
- ✦ When in doubt, drench everything (meats, fruits, veggies) in lime juice.
- ✦ Look for restaurants and street vendors that are clean and relatively bug-free.
- ✦ Drink only purified or bottled water (this includes ice).
- ✦ Unless you're at the beach, wear shoes.
- ✦ Eat your garlic.
- ✦ Wash Your Hands Regularly!

HEALTH INFO:

For more information on international travel and health, see the Center for Disease Control and Prevention's Travelers' Health Web site, www.cdc.gov/travel, or the World Health Organization's similar site, www.who.int/ith/.

MAGAZINES

Longboard Magazine, www.longboardmagazine.com

SG Magazine, www.sgmag.com

Surfer, www.surfermag.com

The Surfer's Journal, www.surfersjournal.com

Surfing, www.surfingthemag.com

Surf Life for Women, www.surflifeforwomen.com

Transworld Surf, www.transworldsurf.com

BOOKS

Frediani, Paul. *Surf Flex*. Long Island City: Getfitnow.com Books, 2001.

Gabbard, Andrea. *Girl in the Curl*. Seattle: Seal Press, 2000.

Kampion, Drew. *The Stormrider Guide North America*. Cornwall: Low Pressure Publications, 2002.

Renneker, Mark and Kevin Starr. *Sick Surfers Ask the Surf Docs and Dr. Geoff*. Boulder, CO: Bull Publishing, 1993.

Snyder, Rocky. *Fit to Surf*. Camden, NJ: Ragged Mountain Press, 2003.

Spacek, Peter. *Wetiquette*. Montauk, NY: Ditch Ink Publishing, 2003.

Sutherland, Bruce. *The World Stormrider Guide*. Cornwall: Low Pressure Publications, 2002.

Warshaw, Matt. *The Encyclopedia of Surfing*. San Diego: Harcourt, 2003.

Weisbecker, Allan C. *In Search of Captain Zero*. New York: J.P. Tarcher, 2002.

CHOICE SURF MOVIES

Aqua Dulce, 2004

Big Wednesday, 1978

Blue Crush, 2002

The Endless Summer, 1966

The Far Shore, 2002

Five Summer Stories, 1972

Focus, 1994

Hit & Run, 2000

Maverick's, 1998

The Modus Mix, 2003

Momentum Three, 2002

North Shore, 1987

Searching for Tom Curren, 1997

September Sessions, 2000

Shutter Speed, 1981

Siestas & Olas, 1997

Step into Liquid, 2003

SURF FORECASTING

www.buoyweather.com

www.fnmoc.navy.mil

www.stormsurf.com

www.surfline.com

ASSOCIATIONS

The Personal

International Women's Surfing (IWS), www.womensurfing.org

The Professional

Association of Surfing Professionals (ASP), www.aspworldtour.com

Eastern Surfing Association (ESA), www.surfesa.org

International Surfing Association (ISA), www.isasurf.org

National Scholastic Surfing Association (NSSA), www.nssa.org

Pro Surfing Tour of America (PSTA), www.prosurfingtour.com

Surfing America, www.surfingamerica.org

The Altruistic

The Ocean Conservancy, www.oceanconservancy.org

Surfrider Foundation, www.surfrider.org

Surf Aid International, www.surfaidinternational.org

CLUBS

Chicks on Sticks, Narragansett, Rhode Island, www.chicksonsticks.org

Coalition of Surfing Clubs, www.surfclubs.org

East Coast Wahines, www.eastcoastwahines.com

Longboard surf clubs and organizations, www.longboard.net/jl_clublist.html

Sisters of the Sea, Neptune Beach, Florida, www.sistersofthesea.org

Wahine Surfing, www.wahinesurfing.com

Women on Board, www.womenonboard.info

SURF PACKAGES AND CHARTERS

Alacran Surf Tours Costa Rica, www.alacransurf.com

Global Surf Travel, www.globalsurftravel.com

Planeta Surf, www.planetasurf.com

Punta Mango Surf Trips, www.puntamango.com

Surf Express, www.surfex.com

Surf Paradise, www.surfparadise.com

Tico Travel, www.ticotravel.com

Waterways Travel, www.waterwaystravel.com

Wavehunters, www.wavehunters.com

Worldwide Adventures, www.worldwideadventures.com

SURF CAMPS/CLINICS

Brazil

Easy Drop, Itacarè, Bahia, www.easydrop.com

California

Girl in the Curl, Dana Point, www.girlinthecurl.com

Santa Cruz Surf School, Santa Cruz, www.santacruzsurfschool.com

Surf Academy, Santa Monica, www.surfacademy.org

Surf City Surfing Lessons, Huntington and Newport Beach, www.dangerwoman.com

Surf Diva Surf School, La Jolla, www.surfdiva.com

Canada

Surf Sister Surf School, Tofino, British Columbia, www.surfsister.com

Costa Rica

Kelea Surf Spa, Malpais, www.keleasurfspa.com

Pura Vida, Malpais, www.puravidaadventures.com

Witch's Rock Surf Camp, Tamarindo, www.witchsrocksurfcamp.com

SURF MAPS

SURF STUFF

✦ Surf-Speak: **The Lingo**

aerial, n: A rather impressive shortboard maneuver in which the surfer launches off the lip of the wave and is momentarily airborne.

angled takeoff, v: To position your board at an angle and take off at that angle.

ASP, n: Association of Surfing Professionals.

backside, adv: Surfing with your back toward the wave.

bail out, v: To dive off your board to avoid a nasty wipeout.

barrel, n: The tubular section of a wave.

barrelled, v: To be inside the tubular section of a wave.

beachbreak, n: Waves that break over a sandbar.

blown-out, adj: When the wind has stirred up the surf so much that the waves are not rideable.

bottom turn, n: A big, powerful turn made at the bottom of the wave.

break, n: A surf spot.

burger or mush burger, n: A mushy, slow-moving wave.

channel, n: An area of deep water where waves don't usually break; great spot to paddle out.

closeout, n: A wave that breaks all at once.

consistent, adj: When waves break with very short lulls in between sets.

cross-step, v: To cross one foot over the other as you work your way up or down a longboard.

curl, n: The area of the wave where it is breaking and spilling over itself.

cutback, n: A turn that takes you back toward the breaking part of the wave.

dawn patrol, n: A sunrise surf session.

deck, n: The top of your board, where you apply the wax and where you stand.

delaminate, v: When the fiberglass separates from the foam of the board; repair if possible.

ding, n: A dent or puncture in your board; must be repaired.

ding, v: To dent or puncture your board.

double-overhead, adj: A measurement used to describe a wave that is twice your size.

double-up, n: A bigger, steeper, thicker breaking wave formed when two smaller waves merge.

drop, n: The initial descent down a wave face after catching a wave.

drop in, v: To catch a wave in front of a surfer who has priority (is closer to the peak); cardinal sin of surfing.

duck-dive, v: You, along with your board, dive under an approaching wave and pop out its backside; shortboard technique.

dude, n: Something you don't call your mom.

face, n: The front of the wave.

fetch, n: The distance along the water's surface over which the wind blows.

fin, n: Located on the underside of the board at the tail; helps you navigate and control the board.

fish, n: A short, flat, wide, stocky board built specifically for waves that are too small and slow to really enjoy with a standard shortboard.

floater, n: A shortboard maneuver where you surf above or "float" the breaking lip.

frontside, adv: Surfing with the front of your body facing the wave.

glassy, adj: When waves are smooth due to little or no wind; a very good thing.

gnarly, adj: A general term for heavy or scary or intense or gross; a wave could be gnarly, a wipeout could be gnarly.

goofyfoot, n: The right-foot-forward surfing stance.

grommet or grom, n: Little kids who surf.

groundswell, n: Ocean swell that is formed by very strong, distant winds; most organized of the swells; big wave potential.

gun, n: A surfboard built for big-wave riding.

hang five, v: To place one foot or five toes just over the nose of your longboard.

hang ten, v: To placing both feet or ten toes just over the nose of your longboard.

haole \how-lē\ n: Hawaiian for a mainlander or nonlocal.

hollow, adj: A type of wave formed when there's a sudden change from deep to shallow water; concave, steep, and fast moving; for advanced surfers only.

impact zone, n: The area where the waves are breaking.

inside, n: The area of the surf where the waves have broken; lots of whitewater.

IWS, n: International Women's Surfing.

kick out, v: To put weight in the back of your board to remove yourself from a wave.

kook, n: An inexperienced or novice surfer; most likely, you.

left, n: A wave that breaks to the left and that you ride to the left.

lineup, n: The area just beyond the breaking waves where surfers assemble to catch waves.

lip, n: The very tip of a cresting wave that's rolling or curling down.

localism, n: When locals are nasty and territorial.

locals, n: People who live near and regularly surf one spot.

lull, n: The downtime between sets.

mushy, adj: A type of wave usually formed when the ocean bottom rises gradually from deep to shallow water; slower moving; not very steep; very forgiving; ideal for beginners.

noseride, v: To surf on the front end of your longboard.

NSSA, n: National Scholastic Surfing Association

offshore wind, n: Wind that blows from the beach onto the surf; can greatly improve the shape of the waves.

onshore wind, n: Wind that blows from the ocean onto shore; can indicate abysmal surf conditions.

outline, n: Another word for the outer shape of the board. It will tell you in general terms how the board will perform in the water.

outside, n: The area of the surf just beyond where the waves are breaking.

overhead, adj: A term used to describe a wave that is over your head.

pack, n: A group of surfers in the lineup.

peak, n: The highest part of the wave and where the wave first breaks.

pearl, v: When the nose of your board submerges.

peel, v: When a wave breaks successively down its face ("peels") as it rolls toward shore.

pintail, n: A type of surfboard tail designed for big, hollow surf. It is pointed, which allows a surfer to hold a line in larger, steeper surf.

pocket, n: The area just beyond the breaking section of a wave; where you want to position yourself and your board on the wave.

pointbreak, n: Surf spot where waves wrap around a point and peel successively down their faces as they roll toward shore.

pop up, v: To explode from prone to standing position once you've caught a wave.

pounded, v: When a wave pummels you after a fall or while paddling out.

punch through, v: To meet a small wave head on and let it rush over you.

push-up, v: A variation of punching through; meet a small wave head on, push yourself up, and let the water rush between you and your board.

quiver, n: A surfer's collection of boards; usually consists of three to ten boards.

rail, n: The rounded edges of your board.

reefbreak, n: Surf spots where the waves break over a rock or coral reef; creates consistently shaped waves.

reform, n: A wave that has broken, returns to a swell, and then breaks again; created when there's a deep trench connecting two shallower sections of ocean bottom; outside and inside waves are potentially surfable.

regularfoot, n: The left-foot-forward surfing stance.

right, n: A wave that breaks to the right and that you ride to the right.

rip current, n: A strong surface current that flows seaward from shore.

rocker, n: The curve of a board; impacts the board's speed as well as its ability to turn.

section, n: A piece of the curl line that drops down ahead of the main area of whitewater.

set, n: A group of bigger-than-average waves rolling toward shore.

shaper, n: Someone who shapes surfboards.

shorebreak, n: *See* beachbreak.

shoulder, n: The unbroken section of the wave.

sideshore wind, n: Wind that blows across the waves; can equate to unpleasant (but bearable) conditions.

skeg, n: *See* fin.

snake, n: Someone who drops in on the priority rider.

snake, v: *See* drop in.

soup, n: *See* whitewater.

squaretail, n: A type of surfboard tail with a square(ish) shape. Designed for everyday conditions.

squashtail, n: A squaretail with soft corners.

stall, v: To rapidly decrease the momentum of a surfboard by putting too much pressure in the tail.

stick, n: Another word for surfboard (disclaimer: use this word only in jest).

stoked, adj: Pumped, happy, excited.

stringer, n: A thin piece of wood (usually basswood or cedar) located in the middle of the board and that runs the length of the board; affects the board's strength and flexibility.

stuff, v: *See* drop in.

swell, n: The long, graceful, uninterrupted lines of energy that you see rolling into shore.

tail, n: The rear section of your surfboard; influences how your board will perform in varying types of surf.

takeoff, n: The initiation (the catching and the popping up) of your dazzling ride.

take off, v: To initiate your dazzling ride.

tide, n: The rising and falling of the ocean's surface.

top turn, n: A turn from the upper section of the wave to the bottom section.

trifin, n: Popular fin configuration; three fins, one fin in the middle and two same-size or smaller fins on either side, a few inches forward of the center fin.

trim, adj: When a board is perfectly balanced so that it planes efficiently and smoothly across the surface of the water.

trim, v: To make slight adjustments of your body weight on your board to keep your board balanced.

trough, n: The bottom portion of a wave.

tube, n: *See* barrel.

turtle roll, n: A longboarding technique in which the surfer flips over her surfboard to more efficiently power through a breaking wave.

wahine, n: A female surfer.

wall, n: The area of the wave face that has yet to break.

WCT, n: World Championship Tour.

whitewater, n: The white, foamy, broken section of the wave.

windswell, n: Ocean swell born of winds that have enough fetch and blow long enough to form rideable waves; disorganized; no detectable swell lines.

wipeout, n: The inevitable fall from grace.

wipe out, v: To fall from grace.

worked, v: When a wave punishes you after a nasty fall.

WQS, n: World Qualifying Series

✦ Contributors

Rochelle Ballard

Barrel queen and surfing legend, Rochelle Ballard, age thirty-three, began surfing when she was eleven. In 1998 and 2001 she was ranked fourth in the world, and in 2003 she placed second at the Billabong Pro Teahupoo and took Surfer Poll's best female performance in a surf video for *Modus Mix*. She has been featured in numerous magazines including *Time*, *Surfing*, *Transworld Surf*, *Surfer*, *SG* magazine, *Sports Illustrated Women*, *National Geographic*, and was a surf stunt double in the 2002 hit movie *Blue Crush*. When not surfing, Rochelle teams with O'Neill to offer surf camps in Hawaii, Florida, and California. She lives in Oahu, Hawaii.

Serena Brooke

Serena, twenty-eight, learned to surf at thirteen. She began competing in the National Scholastic Surfing Association in 1994, was the ASP Rookie of the Year in 1995, won her first World Championship Tour event in 1996, and has ranked in the top fifteen every year since. In 2001 Serena was selected by *Sports Illustrated* as One of the Coolest Women in Sports. She has appeared in numerous magazines and broadcasts, including *SG* magazine, *Surfer*, *Rolling Stone*, *Shape*, *W* magazine, *Sports Illustrated*, ESPN, NBC Sports, Fox Sports Net, ABC Sports, MTV, and National Geographic TV. She lives on the Gold Coast in Queensland, Australia.

Heather Clark

Heather Clark, age thirty-three, has been on the pro circuit for ten years. In 2003 she ranked third in the world, placing second at the Roxy Pro in Fiji, third at the Billabong Pro Teahupoo-Tahiti, the Roxy Pro France, and the Billabong Pro Maui. She has appeared in various surf films including *7 Girls* and publications including *Surf Life for Women* and *Surfer Girl*. Heather, who is goofyfoot, lives in Port Shepstone, South Africa.

Julie Cox

Julie, age twenty-four, first tried surfing when she was eight years old, but she didn't get the full stoke until she was sixteen and could drive herself to the ocean. She began competing at eighteen while pursuing a degree in Environmental Studies at the University of California at Santa Cruz. Julie lives in Agoura Hills, California.

Kim Hamrock

Kim Hamrock, a.k.a "Danger Woman," forty-three, has been surfing for twenty-seven years, and competing for eleven. Her major titles include Women's World Longboard Champion, USA Champion, and West Coast Champion. Kim has been featured in many publications including *Sports Illustrated*, *Surf Life for Women*, *Pacific Longboarder*, *Longboard Magazine*, *Surfer*, *SG* magazine, *Girl in the Curl*, and *The Encyclopedia of Surfing*, as well as television and video productions including Fox Sports Net's *54321*, CNN for Women, the Discovery Channel, *Loose Lips*, *Longboard Magic*, and her own video, *Safe Surfing with Danger Woman*. When not competing, Kim operates her surf school, Surf City Surfing. She lives in Huntington Beach, California.

Margeaux Hamrock

Margeaux Hamrock, age fifteen, has been surfing for twelve years and competing for eleven. In 2002 she was the first place winner at the USA Longboard Championships sixteen-and-under division and second in the West Coast Championships Women's Open. She has appeared in various broadcasts and publications including *Surfer*, *Surf Life for Women*, *SG* magazine, *Surfing*, CNN News, and the ABC Family Channel. Margeaux is the daughter of longboarding legend Kim Hamrock and lives in Huntington Beach, California.

Belen Kimble-Connelly

Belen, twenty-six, grew up in Oceanside and caught the surf bug in high school. She is now considered one of the world's best female longboarders and has appeared in publications including *Rolling Stone*, *Bliss*, *Sports Illustrated for Women*, and *The Surfer's Journal*. She lives half of the year on North Shore, Oahu, and the other half in Australia or on a plane.

Pauline Menczer

Pauline, thirty-four, has been on the pro tour for close to twenty years, has claimed twenty World Championship Tour victories, and was the 1993 world champion. Though she has fought a lifelong battle with rheumatoid arthritis, Pauline consistently ranks in the top ten and continues to push the boundaries of women's surfing. She has appeared many publications including *Girl in the Curl*, *Sports Illustrated*, the *Los Angles Times*, and surf movies such as *Blue Crush* and *Surfabout*. She lives in Byron Bay, Australia.

Mary Osborne

Mary, age twenty-one, picked up her first surfboard at fifteen. In 2003, MTV selected Mary to compete on its new reality series *Surf Girls*, where she won the longboard division. She has appeared on Fox Sports Net's *54321* and has been featured in several magazines including *Longboard Magazine, Surfing, Surfer, Surf Life for Women, SG* magazine, *Nalu, FHM, Entertainment Weekly,* and *Spin* magazine. In 2003 she was chosen as Action Girl of the Year by *SG* magazine. She lives in Ventura, California.

Carla Rowland

Carla Rowland, age twenty-seven, caught the surfing bug when she was fifteen. She was the 2001 MBC Call to the Wall first place winner, and placed second in both the MSA Classic and Women's Longboard Championships in 2002. She has appeared in a number of publications and books including *Longboard, Pacific Longboarder,* and *The Glide,* as well as the films *Loose Lips, Step into Liquid, Multiple Personalities, Reflection,* and others. Rowland, who prefers evening glass to dawn patrol and pointbreaks to beachbreaks, lives in Malibu, California.

Frieda Zamba

Frieda began surfing when she was twelve and by nineteen had won the first of four world titles. Over the course of her ten-year surfing career, Frieda not only dominated the ASP circuit—she had eighteen World Championship Tour wins—but also helped redefine women's surfing. Currently she is working on her own line of surfboards, Zamba, teaches surf lessons up and down the Florida coast, and rides her motorcycle.